Last Things and Last Plays

Shakespearean
Eschatology

Cynthia Marshall

With a Foreword by Arthur F. Kinney

Southern Illinois University Press
Carbondale and Edwardsville

Edited by Rebecca Spears Schwartz
Designed by Shannon M. McIntyre
Production supervised by Natalia Nadraga

94   93   92   91   4   3   2   1

Library of Congress Cataloging-in-Publication Data

Marshall, Cynthia.
    Last things and last plays : Shakespearean eschatology / Cynthia
Marshall : with a foreword by Arthur F. Kinney.
        p.   cm.
    Includes bibliographical references and index.
    1. Shakespeare, William, 1564–1616—Tragicomedies.
    2. Shakespeare, William, 1561–1616—Religion. 3. Christian drama.
English—History and criticism. 4. Eschatology—History of
doctrines—17th century. 5. Eschatology in literature.
    6. Tragicomedy. I. Title.
    PR2981.5 M37   1991
    822.3′3—dc20   90-9883
    ISBN 0-8093-1689-7   CIP

The paper used in this publication meets the minimum requirements
of American National Standard for Information Sciences—Permanence
of Paper for Printed Library Materials, ANSI Z39.48-1984. ⊚

For Anna

Contents

Foreword

"Th'immutable devine decree, which shall / Cause the Worlds End, caus'd his originall": for us, now, Joshua Sylvester's monumental translation of Du Bartas for the English Renaissance would seem to get things backwards. But this is seriously to misundertand the anxieties, caused in part by grave political and religious irreconciliations and in part by an aging queen, that prompted the later Elizabethans (and the early Jacobeans following them) to think hard about the end of things, the end indeed of the world. As early as 1587, William Perkins, that outspoken Puritan leader at Cambridge, published his "Fruitfull Dialogue Concerning The Ende of the World," initiating large numbers of such warnings—first for 1588, then for 1600, then for the Jacobean reign which James I's great Union and new translation of the Bible only seemed to prepare his people to witness—and we find such later poets as Donne and Milton referring quite seriously to "these latter days." Viewed in its own time, Spenser's *Faerie Queene* could be seen not so much as a grand national epic as a testimony to contemporary eschatological issues. The threat of the old queen's death conditioned much of the writing and thinking of the later 1590s; the fact of her death lingered, haunting England (with frequent printed references) well past 1610. This inescapable sense of doom and death, personal and universal both, is surely behind the great tragedies of the period as it is behind the newly emergent (and often bitter) satiric and city comedies. Its pervasive force is felt, too, in the bittersweet romances by which a slightly later age, of the late Shakespeare or of Beaumont and Fletcher, wrote their romances or Jonson his (often overwrought) masques. For Cynthia Marshall, in this thoughtful and provocative book, such a sense ripened and guided Shakespeare's four great romances when re-viewed, in their times and his, as the great playwright's *alterswerk*. Here we find the urgent forces of Shakespeare's time tested by his supreme poetic gift for discipline and exploration: his *alterswerk*, as Marshall points out so forcefully, are identifiable by such standard conventions as an interest in death, a desire for a formal recapitulation, a need for thematic summation. But while they compensate for anxiety by fantasies of renewal and reunion on a grand scale, what Kirby Farrell has called in another new seminal study "play death," death remains, stubbornly and undeniably, the central subject. The possible end of the world, the end of life, the end of a dramatic career of unmatched significance and influence: *Last Things and Last Plays* takes a hard, compelling look at the aging Shakespeare and his late great plays.

Our present-day aging population makes the concerns of Shakespeare's *alterswerk* more poignant, more painful perhaps, surely more apparent for us all. The playwright's personal and professional response, Marshall argues, is fundamentally a familiar one. He questioned, incessantly, the boundaries of his art as the boundaries of life itself: the statue of Hermione in *The Winter's Tale* as a device to confront, probe, frustrate, and finally move his audience; the Baroque attention and sweep of detail by which *Cymbeline* works, endlessly, with life as denouement, unwinding, finishing up; the double perspective of Gower's narration and Shakespeare's drama held together in *Pericles* through the understated but unavoidable review of the ages of history and the ages of man; in *The Tempest*, the life-sustaining forces of Prospero's knowledge of power and power of magic set in dramatic tension with the consequential need to surrender, to let go. (The poetry of George Herbert and the later poetry of Donne will continue this understanding.)

Such redirection of thought can place Shakespeare's last plays in different shades of light, at once revealing their obscurantist leanings towards darkness and watching their more open attempts to confront mortality itself. But what is even more rewarding in Marshall's study is her command of resources. Skillfully here she interweaves official and popular religious treatises with appointed readings in the liturgy of the Established Church and sermons preached at St. Paul's and sold widely there on weekdays. She calls herself "Historicist," and she is well grounded here in authentic documents that, as survivors of their time, help us to recapture what they signify. From the works of

Foreword

George Gifford to those of John Donne the preacher, from the growth of Protestantism (and Puritanism) to the growth of millenarianism, Marshall traces the probing uncertainties of this age of anxiety. But her historicism is as "new" as it is "old," if these labels any longer have meaning, for with the help of such historical documents, she processes Shakespeare's last plays as cultural documents, themselves part of an age that they both reflect and shape. Her wider understanding of cultural forces and human nature allow her to join psychology and history in fruitful ways, and readers will find pregnant conjunctures of Shakespeare's time and our own in a wonderful, mutual interplay: this study also draws on Freud and on Lacan, on seminal thinkers as ranging as Mircea Eliade, Frank Kermode, and Barbara Herrnstein Smith. Such other resources allow Marshall to bring some fresh readings to Shakespeare's understanding, in these last plays, of time, of judgment, of future existence.

Time catches up with Shakepeare in these last days, catches up with his art in these last plays. He is caught, as we all are, sooner or later, with more or less urgency, with the paradoxical, impossible forces of our rational knowledge of the end of life and our desperate need for survival. Early in his career, Shakespeare concentrated on such worries over mortality, too, with his sonnets and plays centering on regeneration through progeny and through the gilded monuments of art. At the end, as Marshall so clearly demonstrates, it was a very different matter, in tone, in substance, in need. The romances with their divided and reconstituted families, their planned patterns for redemption, their desire to reassert self-control over individual destiny and fate, are all what Freud noted as "an inevitable result" of acknowledging the oncoming presence of death; "we should seek in the world of fiction," he writes, "in literature and in the theatre compensation for what has been lost in life." In a culture in which the Apocalypse was common theme and daily subject, Marshall faces squarely what Shakespeare attempts and accomplishes when he acknowledges that his revels, like Prospero's, are now ended. For me, such a perspective adds a new depth of understanding—and of feeling and of beauty—to these works, at once deeply personal and widely cultural; and it makes them closer, and more moving, too.

ARTHUR F. KINNEY

xi

Preface

A few decades ago, literary historians tended to associate apocalypticism primarily with extremist religious groups in Renaissance England. Only recently, thanks in large part to the work of Joseph Wittreich, has there been wide recognition of how thoroughly apocalyptic thought pervaded the culture of England in the sixteenth and seventeenth centuries. The expectation that the end of the world was at hand seems to have been fairly ubiquitous: millenarians, Puritans, Anglicans, and Roman Catholics all shared a concern with last things. Bryan W. Ball states that "belief in an imminent, glorious second advent was widespread across the theological spectrum" and "belong[ed] to the main stream of Christian thought" (46). A prevailing expectation of the world's conclusion would of course have political ramifications in any culture. But these effects were intensified by Elizabethan conceptions of cosmic order. The nature of the world, and of its conclusion, was systematically connected with the nature both of the political or social order and that of the individual creature (Spencer 32). The effects or uses of apocalypticism on the political level have been charted and analyzed by Ball, Wittreich, William Lamont, and Bernard Capp, among others. My own project focuses more on apocalypticism as a concern of individual subjects. However, prevailing Renaissance assumptions of hierarchical order make it impossible to discuss the individual apart from his or her society or universe. In examining what I see as a dialectic between persons and history, though, I have paid less attention to political forces than to individual voices. Drama, I think, asks that we hear such individual voices.

My central contention in this book is that *Pericles, Cymbeline, The Winter's Tale*, and *The Tempest* represent, and to a certain extent epitomize, the eschatological concerns of a culture so heavily imbued with apocalypticism that King James I, speaking in Star Chamber, referred to "the latter days drawing on" (554). Moreover these four plays, considered in themselves, exhibit distinctive qualities of "lastness." The forces shaping the formation of an artistic canon are therefore a preliminary consideration. Although literary biography is not my aim, still there are inherent connections between an author's late works and certain typical thematic concerns, such as death and summation. Of course these concerns are not unique to the Shakespearean canon. But for Shakespeare, their artistic expression reflects the unique conjunction of religious and social forces in Renaissance England. I have used official and popular religious treatises, appointed readings in the Anglican liturgy, and various sermons to formulate the background of eschatological ideas against which the four plays were written. My endeavor is therefore largely historicist in approach. My primary concern, like that of the New Historicism, is to examine how a cultural form, in this case drama, mediates between individuals and established social forces.

I have also used psychoanalytic approaches in treating the issues of artistic creativity raised by the topic. All art, but especially drama, depends for its inception, production, and replication, on a dialectic between individuals and society. The artist carries on tradition even while transforming it through the individual creative act. Watching or even imagining a play, we the audience confront our social selves. In chapter 1, I draw a parallel between this dialectic and the similar one characterizing eschatology. The parallel between drama and eschatology, in many ways the informing motif of the book, is by no means original, as references to the *theatrum mundi* tradition make clear. The idea deserves emphasis, however, in a time like our own when eschatology, if considered at all, tends to be thought of as either an individual *or* a social concern.

Chapters 2 and 3 take as their themes the eschatological subjects of judgment and afterlife. *Cymbeline*, whose connection with the birth of Christ has been recognized, is discussed here as an Advent play. I show how judgment and forgiveness inform the play in various ways and how the final scene offers an image of Apocalypse, the central theme of Advent. An inherent motif in each of Shakespeare's last plays is afterlife—or its corollary in the theater, the return of the dead. The Reformation involved changes in the conception of the afterlife which raised or intensified the question of reunion after death. *The Winter's Tale* addresses with some particularity the question of reunion; the statue scene has relevance to the disputed notions of body-soul dualism and of marriage in heaven.

The last two chapters examine distinctive attitudes toward time, the amorphous raw material to which eschatology attempts to give shape or definition. For the unfolding of its doctrine of patience and hope, *Pericles* depends on a transcendence of time. *The Tempest*, on the other hand, illustrates the basic paradox of Christian notions of temporality—that time moves forward in order to recapture and reform the past. Finally, I show how the various forms of human "ideal worlds" imagined in the Renaissance—paradise, arcadia, utopia—help shape the last plays. Ultimately the theater itself functions as a kind of ideal world, one whose stability derives from an ironic consciousness of its ephemerality and illusoriness.

I am happy to acknowledge debts to Arthur Kirsch, James Nohrnberg, Erik Midelfort, David Lynn, Louise Simons, and John Traverse, all of whom have read some version of the manuscript and all of whom have made helpful suggestions. I want also to thank Carol Burns and Rebecca Schwartz at Southern Illinois University Press, as well as several anonymous readers, for the helpful attention they have given to this book. None of these people, of course, are responsible for whatever errors I have committed. A Faculty Development Grant from Rhodes College funded a summer's work on this book.

I have used G. Blakemore Evans' *Riverside Shakespeare* for quotations throughout. To avoid confusion with my own occasional use of square brackets within quotes, I have silently removed the Riverside brackets. Quotations from the Bible refer to the Geneva version except where otherwise noted. When quoting early texts I have silently emended u/v.

1
Last Things and Last Plays

We transact literature along two of the great axes of human experience,
the line of time and the boundary between self and other.
—Norman Holland, "How Can Dr. Johnson's Remarks on
Cordelia's Death Add to My Own Response?"

As if in the end,
in the marriage with nothingness,
we could ever escape
being absolutely safe.
—Robert Lowell, "The Day"

In her study of *Poetic Closure*, Barbara Herrnstein Smith observes the effectiveness of references to sleep and death as closural devices (102). Allusions to these expected and hence "natural" termination points in human experience can impose a sense of thematic conclusiveness by suggesting the pattern of our own lives. In a sense, such patterns are quite arbitrary, perceived independently from time itself, which passes continuously while we humans come and go. Literary works such as drama and narrative fiction that typically depend upon temporal sequence as a structural principle must therefore find additional means of securing closure. Thus a comedy may trace the course of a love relationship to its perceived "ending," marriage (Barbara Herrnstein Smith 117–18). A wedding will appropriately conclude a courtship and hence a play, but weddings are in themselves arbitrarily scheduled events in the flow of time.

Smith handsomely articulates the basic discrepancies between the way we understand time and the way we understand literature. In this study I will share her assumption that while literature is malleable, time is not, although we almost inevitably impose the shape of our own human experience, which begins and ends, onto our model of time. The book deals with the dominant Christian model of time that supposes time will end as it was created, in a knowable, meaningful, divinely ordained fashion.

1

This model, together with the Renaissance belief in an orderly universe, provided a richly appointed and structured context for thoughts about death and ending. Christian eschatology was itself something of a story in which each individual played a part. It would be nearly impossible for Shakespeare, as an author living in Renaissance England, to avoid drawing connections between the anticipated endings of himself, his works (individually and collectively), and his world.

1

For numerous reasons, most artists reserve full exploration of death through their work until fairly late in their careers. As a result, literary or artistic canons often exhibit thematic closure of a kind similar to that found in individual works. An artist's anxiety about personal mortality may be coupled with the desire for artistic immortality and both feelings exacerbated by fear of the cessation of creative activity. In looking back over his or her oeuvre, the artist may recapitulate earlier modes and directions. Often there is an urge to summarize. Thus three identifiable characteristics of *alterswerk* are interest in death, formal recapitulation, and thematic summation.

Shakespeare's work may seem an exception to the usual rules shaping an artistic canon since his most memorable explorations of personal mortality appear in the tragedies, written at the height of his career. But it has been little noticed that the salient structural and thematic characteristics of the four romances are those of *alterswerk*. Each of the last plays—*Pericles, Cymbeline, The Winter's Tale,* and *The Tempest*—features the apparent death of a central character, and each devotes considerable attention to mourning and loss. The expanded time spans, the resultant muting of emotional tone, and the fantastic plots—formal characteristics of romance as a genre—enable prolonged consideration of themes of death and conclusion. The genre of romance distances both author and audience from the subject of these plays. Yet though it is compensated by fantasies of renewal and reunion, death is the subject.

When a character believed to be dead returns unexpectedly, we might expect the dramatic focus to fall on him or her. Surely such episodes present stunning opportunity to articulate the physical horror of death. The tragic mode would demand, for instance, that Thaisa having been rescued from near death consider, like Hamlet, "the undiscover'd country, from whose bourn / No traveler returns" (*Ham*. 3.1.78–79) or that the heartsick Imogen in *Cymbeline* acknowledge, like Claudio in *Measure for Measure*, a fear "to die, and go we know not where, / To lie in cold obstruction and to rot" (*MM* 3.1.117–18). Mortality instead becomes in the last plays as illusory an event as a character's entrances and exits. The spiritual terror of mortality likewise recedes: the romances contain nothing approaching Lear's experience of being "bound / Upon a wheel of fire" (*Lr*. 4.7.45–46). It seems that death is primarily conceived, from the perspective of romance, as a great divider. But even death's sundering power is limited since the romances posit eventual reunion with those who are lost.

Perhaps most striking about the treatment of death and reunion in Shakespeare's romances is how the interest is directed, in every case, to the haunted reactions of the mourners. Shakespeare probes the responses of Pericles and Leontes when their wives are miraculously returned; Thaisa and Hermione themselves are notably silent. Imogen remarks with seeming taciturnity that she "was dead" (*Cym*. 5.5.259); more highly charged responses to her coma are voiced by Posthumus, Guiderius, and Arviragus. In *The Tempest*, Alonso experiences the death and meaningful recovery of his son while Ferdinand himself wanders the island giddily but safely. The significance of death in these four plays is distinctly social. Rather than concentrating on the abstract metaphysics of bodily expiration (as in *Hamlet* and *Measure for Measure*) or the theology of damnation and redemption (as in *King Lear* and *Macbeth*), the last plays attend primarily to mortality's consequences for the human community. The social emphasis dictates not only the motif of reunion present in each play, but also the exploration of judgment in *Cymbeline*, the demand for reassessment in *Pericles*, and the drive toward forgiveness in *The Tempest*.

Yet no matter what social lens mortality is viewed through, death is, at center, a personal concern. Personal mortality has the strange capacity to become raw material for what may be the author's larger, related concern: artistic immortality. To remain alive as an artist means continuing to produce, but in a world whose subjects are finite, this entails learning to begin again, to return to the past, and as Yeats did, to "enumerate old themes"

3

(336). Yeats expresses ambivalence about returning to the past. To him, the act seems to signal loss of creativity, even though its result is the "Circus Animals' Desertion." Nineteenth-century critics who labeled Shakespeare's last plays the products of an imagination grown senile recognized, at least, the recapitulatory quality that *Pericles, Cymbeline, The Winter's Tale,* and *The Tempest* share with other *alterswerk.* As in dreams or remembrances, echoes and images from earlier experiences—earlier plays—fade in and out of focus. Jachimo's resemblance to Iago, Prospero's similarity to the Duke of *Measure for Measure,* Leontes' likeness to Othello—all are obvious. The author's past, which we share through his work, is returning in the late plays. Once again Shakespeare works through the psychology of temptation, the ruler's struggle for personal justice, the pathology of sexual jealousy. Central preoccupations take on their final, if not their perfect, shape.

In itself recapitulation has little artistic worth. When coupled with a summary impulse, it can uncover or describe an inclusive pattern that shapes an artist's works into a new and meaningful whole. David Grene identifies a common theme in the last plays of Ibsen, Sophocles, and Shakespeare: "the establishment of meaning for the events of a life, looking backward from its conclusion" (vii). The paradigmatic summary vision in our culture is the biblical Apocalypse, the Book of the Revelation of Saint John the Divine. This final work achieves conclusiveness by suggesting a summary of the biblical message ("a mosaic of allusions to the Old Testament," writes Northrop Frye [*Great Code* 135], and to the New Testament as well) and by concurrently projecting a prophetic vision of the world's conclusion. The Apocalypse is thus poised between literary and historical past, and prophesied future; it manages paradoxically to contain both past and future, and hence all time. Simple recapitulation thus yields to summation.

In Shakespeare's last plays, the impulse to "establish meaning for the events of a life" takes two forms: incessant questioning of the boundaries of art and life, and expansion of the tragic frame to accommodate the perspective of romance. The statue of Hermione probes the capacity of art to move and to frustrate the theater audience. *Cymbeline* with its Baroque attention to detail, *The Tempest* with its flaunted adherence to the dramatic unities, and *Pericles* with the double fictionality provided by

4

Gower's perspective also stretch the parameters of art. Each play, moreover, presents the structural riddle of tragedy contained by romance. As David Scott Kastan puts it, "Seemingly tragic events are seen to participate in a divine comedy" (29). One significant result of that structure is the devotion paid to time itself as a power in human affairs (Peterson 8). In each play, time is transcended in some way.

2

These three characteristics of *alterswerk*—interest in death, recapitulation, and summation—identify not only finality in artistic canons, but thoughts about finality in general. These same characteristics describe eschatology, the wider field to which *alterswerk* belong. Shakespeare's last plays share with the biblical Apocalypse the broad structural similarities of recapitulation and summation. But the romances are not prophetic in the ordinary sense, and they are not overtly apocalyptic. Nevertheless, in a distinctive way they address the same question that inspires the biblical Apocalypse: what is the meaning of ending? Turning on a crucial dialectic between two perceptions of ending—the death of the individual and the death of the world—eschatology (as it was understood in Renaissance England)[1] parallels and predicts the direction of Shakespeare's imagination at the end of his career. "What human need can be more profound than to humanize the common death?" Frank Kermode has asked (*Ending* 7). Shakespeare implicitly answers by transmuting private concerns into drama, illustrating in the process the preoccupations with judgment and afterlife that had led to traditional Christian eschatology.

However, it looks as though Shakespeare's fit with the Christian eschatology of his day was not perfect. At certain points the

1. I use the term *eschatology* to encompass the complex system of ideas about last things, even though the term itself was not used in the Renaissance. According to *The Oxford English Dictionary [OED]*, *eschatology*, from the Greek *eschatos*, meaning *last*, dates from the middle of the nineteenth century. In contrast to *apocalypticism*, which refers to revelation or expectation of the world's end, *eschatology* suggests more widely the personal, social, and historical attitudes and approaches toward ultimate things, including death and apocalypse.

plays differ in fairly radical ways from orthodox Anglican notions of the last things. Shakespeare's relationship to the culture of his age is obviously crucial in a study such as this one, and in exploring that relationship, I find my work to be aligned in some ways with the current New Historicism. I understand three basic levels of complexity possible in the relationship between an artist and his or her culture. The simplest formulation perceives an artist's connection with an age to be essentially passive: all art bears the imprint of its historical epoch, but great art is that in which this imprint is most deeply marked. E. M. W. Tillyard's *Elizabethan World Picture* exemplifies this approach to Shakespearean criticism, and despite the disfavor into which Tillyard's theory has fallen, all cultural studies in some way share its most basic assumption, that literature is embedded in a particular culture. The rival demands of revenge and Christian mercy can be said in a sense to produce *Hamlet,* and Shakespeare's culture, not Shakespeare, establishes such demands.

A more dynamic sense of the interaction between artist and age realizes art's shaping power. Lawrence Lipking notes, for example, how "a mighty poet gathers his strength by embodying the essential thought of his age" (9). Shakespeare's plays have been widely understood to be not simply reflections of a world picture, but the primary cultural artifacts illuminating, or even producing, that picture. Hence the current trend among some feminist and Marxist critics is to interrogate Shakespeare's patriarchal, capitalistic societal structures. But as Stephen Greenblatt and, more emphatically, Jonathan Dollimore have shown, drama is uniquely able to bear a heterodox and even radical relationship to many facets of a particular society and yet remain firmly fixed within that society. Accordingly, the traditional conception of Shakespeare as spokesman for his age (and even for all time) has expanded to include other roles, notably those of critic, reactionary, and prophet.

It is useful to amplify a theoretical notion of the political relationship between an author and an age with a psychological approach, which, though constrained, is less purely contingent upon history. Otto Rank, investigating the sources of artistic creativity, identifies two compelling and necessarily convergent desires: the artist's wish to achieve personal immortality through creative work, and confirmation of the culture's "collective immortality-idea" (14). Rank's theory of creativity is thus founded on what he calls the "fundamental dualism of all life," that existing between "the individual and the collective, the personal and the social" (xxii). A dualistic theory of creativity helps to explain how a single artist can achieve the stature of Shakespeare, who seems not only to manifest his particular age (which was by no means monolithic) but also to encompass the competing elements whose ongoing dialogue constitutes a culture, which is now in part our culture. Moreover, Rank's theory is particularly relevant to the creation of last works, in which, as Lipking, Grene, and others have pointed out, both personal mortality and artistic immortality are at stake. But most strongly to the point is the inherent connection between Rank's "fundamental dualism" and eschatology, for every consideration of "last things" in some way asks the question, "What lasts when I end?"

In our own day, given increasing focus on the individual and the absence in our culture of a strongly realized communal religion, it is easy to think of death and eschatology as separate concepts, to contrast the certainty of personal extinction with a mere anxiety about universal extinction. Relatively few people in modern America adhere to the doctrine of the literal Apocalypse that formed the core of early seventeenth-century eschatology. In Shakespeare's England, the expectation that Christ would return to earth, raise the dead, pronounce judgment, and lead the blessed into the New Jerusalem was widely discussed and "unanimously accepted" by "orthodox circles as the literal truth" (Patrides 174). Today's "modern apologists of the faith," on the other hand, tend "to regard the Second Advent and the accompanying Universal Resurrection, Last Judgment and Final Conflagration as 'symbols' of the actual last events of history" (Patrides 174). Even in Shakespeare's day it was understood that when an official mythology ceased to be believed literally, it might still retain currency as image or symbol. And in fact, Shakespeare's romances are crucially positioned in Christian history: the literal nature of the Apocalypse, universal resurrection, and afterlife had begun to be questioned. It was probably not coincidental that as these theological doctrines were being scrutinized in new ways, they were also being dramatized in new ways. This transformation of doctrine into metaphor forms a crucial part of my argument.

3

Through the doctrine of Judgment Day, Renaissance eschatology acknowledged the collectivity of humankind. Although orthodox theology maintained that each individual's fate was resolved at the moment of his or her death, universal judgment was still a necessary part of the divine order. Elnathan Parr in 1615 wrote:

> There must be a generall Judgement notwithstanding [previous individual judgments], both that the justnesse of such particular Judgement may bee made more manifest to the glory of God, and that the whole man, consisting of body and soule, may receive the due reward. (280)

The general judgment would resolve any apparent discrepancies between the judgment of an individual and the final configuration of society, and it would confirm in each person the union of body and soul. Judgment Day would thus heal the tensions and dualities of earthly creation.

Theological discussions of eschatology usually make reference to a dialectic between individuals and society. Eschatology may in fact be most simply defined as a way of viewing collectively what we each experience singly—death. But it is also possible to find in the hermeneutics of eschatology a resolution, which Elnathan Parr hints at, between two sorts of dualistic thinking: the primal division of soul and body, and the social distinction of individual and group. The problem is one defined by contemporary theologian Karl Rahner when he writes of how a person "is always a unique spiritual being 'subsisting in himself' " while "also a social entity of the world, 'subsisting in matter' " ("Parousia" 459). It is the private self to which individuals in our culture have been taught to grant immortal existence; we cannot well imagine ourselves ceasing to exist, and in this sense, we identify and imagine ourselves actually to be our ghostly or spiritual selves. But we are known in the world as bodily creatures, and while we see that bodies do end, we see also that the social world continues regardlessly.

Endings can be definitive in other ways, however, which are not so immediately obvious. Human death, even if it is meaningless in itself, is more than the last event in a temporal sequence, for a meaningless consummation would endorse, and therefore confirm, the meaninglessness of the whole. The same can certainly be said for the death of the world. The last things are therefore disproportionately loaded with meaning. It is in this sense that Rahner finds in eschatology the apex and fulfillment of the various dialectics that inform existence:

> Man as a corporeal, historical reality and man as a transcendental, personal spirit; man as an individual and man as a member of the human race, as a member of a collective reality; man as spiritual person and man as a reality to whom there necessarily belongs a world as the milieu and environment in which he actualizes his existence: all of these statements in their plurality are the presuppositions for eschatological statements. . . . There is necessarily an *individual* and a *collective* eschatology, not as statements about disparate realities, but rather as statements about each concrete person himself. (*Foundations* 444)

Judgment Day is understood by Rahner, as it was in the Renaissance, not as a separate event, a "disparate reality," but as the expression of a crucial facet of human identity. In this Christian version of history, each individual dies at a particular moment, but because each individual composes a more or less important part of both society and species, his or her life will not be ultimately completed until the world ends.

A close analogy exists between the individual and communal interpretations of eschatology and the personal and social tensions of drama. Rahner adopts the metaphor with a force of seeming inevitability:

> After individuals have played their role here, they do not depart from a drama which as a whole continues on endlessly, a drama which continues to give spiritual individuals the possibility of performing their act on a stage which has been erected permanently. The *whole* is a drama, and the stage itself is also part of it. (*Foundations* 446)

In recognizing the theatricality of eschatology, its freighting of spectacle with meaning, its interweaving of personal and social identity, Rahner acknowledges the traditional conception of the *theatrum mundi*. Behind the topos lies the medieval idea of human history as "the artifact of God . . . shaped by Him and express[ing] His truth" (Kolve 122). The theatrical model was very widely used in the Renaissance. The appearance of Thomas Beard's *Theatre of Gods Judgements* four times between 1597 and 1648 suggests the appeal of the title alone. John Donne wrote that "our sight of God here, our Theatre, the place where we sit and see him, is the whole world, the whole house and frame of nature" (*Sermons* 8: 220). The metaphor appeared in apocalyptic tracts such as that of John Harvey, who warned of "so notable a *Tragedie* . . . as hath not often beene plaied upon this mortall stage, and fraile *Theater*" (130). According to the medieval and Renaissance notion of the *theatrum mundi*, human time was the theater, God was the playwright, and the Apocalypse would be God's last and greatest play.

4

Much has been written of the apocalyptic impact of Prospero's revels speech, and of the richness of its ambiguous references to stage and to life. If human history exists but as an "insubstantial pageant," then history's conclusion—its moment of dissolution—will be the climax of that drama:

> Our revels now are ended. These our actors
> (As I foretold you) were all spirits, and
> Are melted into air, into thin air,
> And like the baseless fabric of this vision,
> The cloud-capp'd tow'rs, the gorgeous palaces,
> The solemn temples, the great globe itself,
> Yea, all which it inherit, shall dissolve,
> And like this insubstantial pageant faded
> Leave not a rack behind.
> (*Tmp.* 4.1.148–56)

Prospero mentions no author for "this vision," but the speech asks to be understood anagogically, with Shakespeare as author for the vision in the Globe Theater and God as author for that of the earthly globe. The speech advertises the connections between individual, artistic, and universal conclusions. Ironically, however, the transcendent moment yields to the world of everyday responsibilities; Prospero, needing to attend to Caliban's plot,

10

cannot sustain an abstract vision of the dissolution of the world. Neither, it would seem, can Shakespeare or his audience train the focus consistently on metaphysical speculation. So while the mystical and esoteric components of traditional eschatology exert their fascination throughout the last plays, influencing structure, theme, and imagery, Shakespeare distinctly modifies these traditions, to acknowledge the theater's most compelling reality—the bodies and voices of individual persons.

2
Advent and Apocalypse in Cymbeline

"If you can't believe you're going to heaven in your own body and on a first-name basis with all the members of your family, then what's the point of dying?"
—Joan Didion, The White Album

"Th'immutable devine decree, which shall / Cause the Worlds End, caus'd his originall" (Du Bartas 2). As these lines from Du Bartas' creation narrative suggest, Christian eschatology was based on the notion that the world's ending was implicit in its beginning. From a theological standpoint, the birth of Christ established a structure in history that would lead inevitably to Judgment Day. Since the liturgical year was designed to suggest, within its annual cycle, the greater course of Christian history, the beginning of the Church year—Advent—was haunted by endings. On the first Sunday of Advent, Anglicans prayed for grace, being mindful of "the last day, when he shall come in glorious majesty to judge both the quick and the dead" (*Book of Common Prayer [BCP]* 77). For four penitential weeks, the apocalyptic note was sounded. Appointed readings, such as the portents of doom described in Luke 21, trained the congregation's thoughts forward toward the world's last day. Other lessons ("judge nothing before the time" [*BCP* 81], "love thy neighbor as thyself" [*BCP* 77]) underscored a practical application of apocalypticism, teaching that in the face of the final judgment no one is worthy, and charging the congregation to show forgiveness so they might hope to receive it. The concern with endings was underscored by traditional use of the Litany during Advent, with its reiterated plea for deliverance (e.g., "From lightning and tempest, from plague, pestilence, and famine, from battle and murder, and from sudden death[,] Good Lord deliver us" [*BCP* 69]). The Advent focus on the Apocalypse elaborated connections between the death of each individual and the death of the world.[1]

It was fairly well known in the Renaissance that King Cymbeline's reign coincided historically with the time of Christ's birth. A number of critics have found in the historical coincidence a useful key to the play's action. Robin Moffet, for instance, describes *Cymbeline* as "striving after union," its plot and its themes seeking a "centre" which is "assumed as shortly to take place" (218), in the Incarnation. It is helpful to discover an external gloss for an unruly play, but in order to pursue the connection adequately, it is necessary to explore prevailing Renaissance attitudes toward the time surrounding Christ's birth. *Cymbeline* scarcely fits modern secular notions of the Nativity. The play is not hopeful, certainly not celebratory. If we consider, however, the traditional tone of Advent, the way the liturgical season was regarded in the early seventeenth century, we see that *Cymbeline* anticipates the Nativity in a similar way—by brooding on death, judgment, and apocalypse.[2]

Attention to death in this play takes a curious form: the lovely funeral rites for comatose Imogen are juxtaposed with the grotesque attention paid to headless Cloten. Issues of judgment

---

1. Advent retains these characteristics in the Anglican Church. I use the past tense here to historicize references to the Elizabethan prayer book.

2. Given the play's thematic appropriateness for Advent, the connection would of course be strengthened by external evidence linking the play with the liturgical season. No extant records indicate that *Cymbeline* was either commissioned or selected for court performance during Advent. But indeed, since Advent was a penitential season, such a production would be unlikely since most court performances were scheduled on festival days clustered around Christmas and Easter. From contemporary account, however, we know that *Cymbeline* was performed at court during the Christmas season, "on Wensday night the first of January, 1633[/4]" (Bentley 1: 127). The scriptural lesson appointed for 1 January, New Year's Day, includes a verse from Romans that is strongly apposite to *Cymbeline:* "Therefore thou art inexcusable, o man, whosoever thou art that judgest: for in that thou judgest another, thou condemnest thy self: for thou that judgest, doest the same things" (Romans 2.1). However minor, this association of the play with secular New Year's Day—also an occasion for reassessment, judgment, and fresh beginning—contributes to a link with the judgmental motif of Advent.

inform the play's three plots: Cymbeline's broken relationship with Rome, Posthumus' mistreatment of Imogen, and Belarius' abduction of Cymbeline's sons. The numerous plot strands are resolved in a huge final recognition scene whose apocalyptic ramifications deserve attention. The play's concern with judgment, its image of the way death robs human identity, and its culminating apocalyptic scene manifest an eschatological inquiry into the bonds between the individual and society.[3] The play illustrates the individual understanding of eschatology by presenting concrete images of death, which remind the audience of their personal mortality. It illustrates communal eschatology by suggesting a last day on which "the private should be judged"; Doomsday was ordained, according to Jeremy Taylor, so that "every word and every action shall receive its just recompense of reward" ("Advent" 8). Each eschatological motif in *Cymbeline*—death, judgment, and apocalypse—is comprehended in both individual and communal senses.

1

Cymbeline has not typically been thought of as a play about death. Yet the list Robert Uphaus assembles to illustrate the "conspicuous" presence of death or the threat of death in the play is impressive:

> The queen, who wishes to kill Imogen, Pisanio, and Cymbeline, herself dies at the end of the play; Cloten wants to kill Posthumus and rape Imogen; Posthumus wants Pisanio to kill Imogen; Cloten is dead; Imogen is thought to be dead; Cymbeline believes his sons to be dead; the war between Britain and Rome promises death; Posthumus wants to be executed; Cymbeline wants to kill Iachimo, and unknowingly condemns his own son, disguised as

3. Lila Geller identifies *Cymbeline* as a play especially concerned with covenants connecting people in the familial, political, and religious dimensions (254). Meredith Skura writes that *Cymbeline* is "about several different relationships that hold men together. Its three main plots examine political, generational or familial, and maritial ties" ("Interpreting" 207). David Scott Kastan finds the "pattern of innocence/fall/redemption" in each of the three plots (147).

14

Guiderius, for the death of Cloten. So the plot of the play, to the point of excess, is garbed in death. (59–60)

Uphaus, anxious to assimilate the play to his own model of "romance," labels *Cymbeline* a parody—"structurally a romance that experientially does not feel like one" (60). The play's wrenching of generic (and emotional) gears is in fact characteristic of tragicomedy. But *Cymbeline* is exceptional in its emphasis on purely physical aspects of destruction and decay. The play draws attention to the physicality of its own medium in order to demonstrate something about "what mortality is" (4.1.15).

It is Cloten, the buffoon of the play, who initiates *Cymbeline*'s strange funeral sequence. His uncharacteristically profound remark—"What mortality is!"—occurs in the context of the soliloquy in which he announces his violent plan to rape Imogen. Cloten is obsessed by his physical resemblance to Imogen's husband, Posthumus: "the lines of my body are as well drawn as his" (4.1.9–10). The physical similarity allows Cloten and Posthumus to function as psychomachic doubles, as recent criticism has shown.[4] But it also has powerful thematic resonance: the resemblance of the two men illustrates the common leveling power of death. And it helps prepare for the lesson about the mutuality of judgment ("thou that judgest, doest the same things" [Romans 2.1]). Cloten in fact speaks like a prophet, for the audience soon sees how ephemeral mortality is: Cloten is beheaded in the next scene. Moreover, when Imogen herself mistakes "the lines of [Cloten's] body" for those of Posthumus', the transience of human identity is compellingly illustrated.

Imogen offers the refrain to Cloten's reference to mortality when she says, just fifteen lines later:

> But clay and clay differs in dignity,
> Whose dust is both alike.
> (4.2.4–5)

---

4. Arthur Kirsch shows how Cloten functions as Posthumus' psychological double. The beheading of Cloten symbolically resolves the troubled aspects of the hero that prompted his jealousy and aggression (156–60). Joan Carr remarks how "Cloten seems to be a grotesque projection, and yet not all that much of an exaggeration, of the very worst elements in Posthumus' nature" (320). Ruth Nevo maintains that "both Cloten and his counterpart Iachimo . . . represent isolated and split-off parts of an ambivalent and unintegrated personality" (75).

Echoing the memorable phrase from the Anglican burial service, "earth to earth, ashes to ashes, dust to dust" (*BCP* 310), Imogen's speech sets a solemn tone for the scene in which Cloten will be beheaded, and she will appear to die after swallowing the queen's drug.

The tone of the scene, however, is complex and by no means simply funereal. Imogen's death is mistaken, and Cloten's beheading seems peculiarly designed to parry the audience's sympathy. The boasting of Guiderius ("Not Hercules / Could have knock'd out his [Cloten's] brains, for he had none" [4.2.114–15]), the envy of Arviragus ("Would I had done't" [156]), and the final dispatching of "Cloten's clotpole down the stream" (184) effectively transform his death into semicomic spectacle. Cloten in this regard resembles Antigonus in *The Winter's Tale*, whose "*Exit pursued by a bear* " (3.3.58sd) is at once humorous, tragic, grotesque, and expedient. Each character functions like an emotional decoy, whose death allows the audience to acknowledge mortality without feeling grief.

The presence of death in *Cymbeline* has been little remarked, I think, precisely because of the emotional distancing produced by odd discrepancies of tone and by layered artifice of technique. The play's self-conscious artifice—what Granville-Barker describes as "art, which deliberately displays its art" (467)—prevents the audience from becoming viscerally involved. We might consider, for instance, the way Arviragus reports Imogen's death: he lingers lovingly over minute descriptive details. Imogen, disguised as Fidele, was discovered

> stark, as you see:
> Thus smiling, as some fly had tickled slumber,
> Not as death's dart being laugh'd at; his right cheek
> Reposing on a cushion.
> . . . .
>   O' th' floor;
> His arms thus leagu'd. I thought he slept, and put
> My clouted brogues from off my feet, whose rudeness
> Answer'd my steps too loud.
>
>   (4.2.209–15)

The palpable details contribute to the verse's rich texture, but they also draw attention to the poetic medium itself. Even his brother becomes impatient with Arviragus' effusiveness, begging him, after an extended discussion of funeral flowers, to

> have done,
> And do not play in wench-like words with that
> Which is so serious.
>
> (4.2.229–31)

The verbal picture of Imogen, and in fact the entire episode of her supposed death and burial, is exaggerated in the style of a Mannerist painting to the point of being self-consciously illusory. The technique complicates an audience's relationship with events on stage, creating an emotional distance which isolates the presented image—in this case, the image of dead Imogen.

Most funerals call attention to the dead body, either explicitly or implicitly. The rites performed for Imogen and Cloten are no exception. Because theirs is a double funeral, and especially because Imogen and Cloten are held in such different regard, the commonality of death, its leveling power, is illustrated. Belarius says the "mean and mighty, rotting / Together, have one dust" (4.2.246–47); Guiderius responds in kind that "Thersites' body is as good as Ajax', / When neither are alive" (4.2.252–53). These remarks, along with the refrain of the funeral song, "all must . . . come to dust," and Belarius' pronouncement that "the ground that gave them first has them again" (4.2.289), echo the theme initiated by Imogen: "dust thou art and unto dust shalt thou return." In the pre-Christian world of the play, no mention is made of afterlife, immortality, or deity; the absence of spiritual consolation heightens the main theme—corporeal death. The subdued but recurrent echo from the Anglican burial service, an example of Shakespearean anachronism, might suggest to the Renaissance audience a contrast between the finality of pagan death and the hope of afterlife associated with Christian burials.

The play's characteristically insistent attention to physicality hovers between the grotesque and the comical when Imogen awakens to discover the headless Cloten beside her. Granville-Barker, declaring the scene "fraud on Imogen," bemoans the way "we are accomplices" as she "is put, quite needlessly, quite heartlessly, on exhibition" (539). In contrast to her romance counterparts, Thaisa and Hermione, each of whom awakens from supposed death to a group of loving supporters, Imogen arises, like Juliet, alone, terrified, and confronted by a dead body. The irony is painful as Imogen confirms that, in fact, "Thersites' body is as good as Ajax'," or Cloten's as good as Posthumus', "when neither are alive." However awkward the moment for Imogen (or for the actress playing Imogen), the scene provides stunning evidence of death's reductive power.

Given the lesson the scene illustrates, it is odd that critics have concentrated on Imogen's inability to recognize her husband's body, rather than on the sheer carnality of the episode. Embarrassment for Imogen aside, her enumeration of bodily parts as she gropes the length of the corpse is powerfully disconcerting:

> I know the shape of 's leg; this is his hand,
> His foot Mercurial, his Martial thigh,
> The brawns of Hercules; but his Jovial face—
> Murther in heaven? How? 'Tis gone.
> (4.2.308–12)

The deific adjectives express her spiritual idealization of Posthumus, but the described action is explicitly physical and implicitly sexual. It corresponds closely with the Hostess' description of the death of Falstaff in *Henry V:*

> I put my hand into the bed and felt [his feet], and
> they were as cold as any stone; then I felt to his knees,
> and so up'ard and up'ard, and all was as cold as any
> stone.
> (*H5.* 2.3.23–26)

Yet even the Hostess, who is coarse, earthy, and perfectly aware of whose body she touches, only narrates the action and does not perform it on stage. The displaced sexual innuendoes of Imogen's "necrophilic embrace" have quite rightly received attention. Michael Taylor writes of the "mad burlesque of sexual passion and shattered idyllic expectations" (99). But as the startling culmination of the play's lesson about mortality, the scene offers more than a "grotesque . . . climax to the play's pastoral activity" (Michael Taylor 98): it offers an ontological lesson on human identity and its reduction to flesh. Cloten's body, considered without its head, not only resembles Posthumus' body but becomes, in a sense, its equivalent. As Robert Hunter puts it, "Cloten is quite right [about his physical resemblance to Posthumus]. As a thing, he is the equal of Posthumus, and Posthumus has chosen, for the time, to change himself into a thing" (158). This confusion of Cloten's and Posthumus' common hardware presents a galling illustration of death's capacity to rob significant distinctions between one person and another. *Cymbeline's* funeral sequence offers a specific instance of the way buffoon and hero, king and beggar, end as mere bodies. The romance illustrates Hamlet's perception of how "we fat ourselves for maggots" (*Ham.* 4.3.22–23).

When, during Advent, the Church taught the terror of Judgment Day, its purpose was to point the contrast between Christian and pre-Christian views of the end of the world. In the four weeks preceding Christmas, the congregation was meant to experience the dark of the centuries before Christ. The pagan ontology of death in *Cymbeline*, its utter denial of spiritual consolation, contrasts with a religious hope of afterlife. The difference is less obvious in our largely secular age than it would have been in Renaissance England. With its enactment of raw, physical tragicomedy, the funeral sequence in *Cymbeline* suggests a pre-Christian era in which there is no apparent possibility of spiritual enlightenment.

2

Cloten's soliloquy at the beginning of act 4 of *Cymbeline* introduces a sequence focused on physical mortality. The structural parallel of his speech is the one Posthumus delivers at the start of act 5, when he returns to stage after being absent for two acts. During the interval of his absence, Posthumus, duped into thinking his wife unfaithful, has sent orders for her to be killed. He enters, overwhelmed with guilt and remorse, planning to fight in Britain's defense by way of atonement. Whereas Cloten's soliloquy inaugurates attention to death, Posthumus' speech initiates the play's most concentrated and individuated treatment of judgment. The parallel speeches further the antithetical characters of Cloten and Posthumus, illustrating the way they function as psychomachic counterparts. The two speeches also introduce two major, interrelated thematic excursions in the play.

When Posthumus turns up outside the Roman camp, he is unaware that Pisanio has disobeyed the order to kill Imogen and has sent a false token. He addresses the token and then the audience:

> Yea, bloody cloth, I'll keep thee, for I wish'd
> Thou should'st be colour'd thus. You married ones,
> If each of you should take this course, how many
> Must murther wives much better than themselves
> For wrying but a little! O Pisanio,
> Every good servant does not all commands;
> No bond, but to do just ones. Gods, if you
> Should have ta'en vengeance on my faults, I never
> Had liv'd to put on this; so had you saved
> The noble Imogen to repent, and strook
> Me, wretch, more worth your vengeance.
>   (5.1.1–11)

Judged on intentions, he is guilty of his wife's murder, and critical reaction to Posthumus at this point generally endorses his scathing self-indictment. The situation is complicated by Posthumus' still believing that Imogen has cuckolded him. Nevertheless, he now dismisses her supposed infidelity as "wrying but a little." Would he be so magnanimous if he did not think her dead? Othello is likewise sorry that he killed his wife, but the tragic hero gives no hint that he would have behaved differently if Desdemona had actually been Cassio's lover (Grene 56). Even the fifteen-year penitent Leontes does not suggest that he would forgive Hermione had she actually been unfaithful; he realizes instead that his own perceptions were mistaken. Posthumus' forgiveness therefore violates the norms for Renaissance drama, where honor is typically the code which regulates sexual behavior. His attitude here, as Joan Carr writes, "parallels the Christian doctrine of forgiveness: 'Love your enemies, do good to them that hate you' " (321). Importation of the religious ethic into the manifestly secular plot of Posthumus' sexual jealousy is unexpected, but in keeping with the largest concerns of the play.

Robert Hunter, who sees Posthumus as "the central, *humanum genus* figure of the play" (143), describes the character's crucial inner turn toward self-knowledge: "Self-knowledge must necessarily be a knowledge of sinfulness, and it will lead to remorse and the forgiveness of a wife who, he thinks, has wronged him" (161). Posthumus achieves a perspective from which recognition of common sinfulness allows for mutual forgiveness. The desirability of such knowledge and such forgiveness was reiterated throughout Advent, as the following selections from the appointed readings illustrate:

> Owe nothing to any man but this, that ye love one another.
> For he that loveth another, fulfilleth the law. (*BCP* 77)

> The God of patience and consolation, grant you to be like-
> minded one toward another. . . . (*BCP* 78)

> With me it is but a very small thing that I should be judged
> of you, either of man's judgment: no, I judge not mine own
> self; for I know nought by myself, yet am I not thereby
> justified. It is the Lord that judgeth me. (*BCP* 80–81)

These verses are informed not only by Christian humility, but
by a precise condemnation of judgment. I would extend Hunter's
argument that Posthumus learns charity (159) by pointing out
the play's emphasis on what Posthumus must concurrently give
up: his self-righteousness.

Advent, with its recurrent consideration of the Apocalypse,
presented the Church with a tremendous opportunity to enforce
its moral code. Theologians heightened the terror of Judgment
Day in order to inspire self-scrutiny. Thus George Gifford
warned in a sermon that on the last day

> all the filthie uncleannes of mens hearts shall lie open to
> the viewe of men and angels, and their owne conscience
> shall then shew unto them their deeds, their words, and
> their wicked thoughts. Then shall their inwards be as it
> were displayed. (406)

Gifford projects a final effacement of distinction between private
and public realms. To heighten the rhetorical as well as the
doctrinal effect, he assumes that the inward self is necessarily
shameful. In a widely read tract, *A Woorke Concerning the trewnesse
of the Christian Religion* (translated into English in 1587 by Sir
Philip Sidney and Arthur Golding), Philippe de Mornay also
noted the inward emphasis of the final judgment. Intentions
would matter as much as deeds:

> Gods giving of his Lawe, not to the outward man but to the
> inward, nor to our deedes only but also to our thoughts,
> sheweth sufficiently . . . that there is another Judge than
> the Magistrats of this world to judge us, and another Judg-

21

ment than their judgement [sic]. . . . Neither would our
owne consciences sumon us so often as they do, if we were
not to appeare before other than men. (639)

Emphasis on the inescapability of a judgment that would extend
to thoughts as well as deeds was meant to promote good behavior
and clean consciences. But in order to discourage self-righteousness and to inspire charity, a sense of collective sin and universal
trembling before "another Judgment" was tapped.

Posthumus' soliloquy gives extreme, even exaggerated, expression to such ideas. Addressing the theater audience, he
insists that sinfulness is inherent in the human condition:

> You married ones,
> If each of you should take this course, how many
> Must murther wives much better than themselves
> For wrying but a little!
>
> (5.1.2–5)

The assumption of marital infidelity and the astonishing (in this
context) denial of its importance challenge accepted codes of
behavior. Posthumus is searching, reaching for an understanding of divine judgments. He addresses the gods:

> But alack,
> You snatch some hence for little faults; that's love,
> To have them fall no more: you some permit
> To second ills with ills, each elder worse,
> And make them dread it, to the doers' thrift.
>
> (5.1.11–15)

Although he then prays to be made an instrument of the gods
("do your best wills, / And make me blest to obey" [5.1.16–17]),
his presumption of the ability to measure faults and to discern
divine purposes reveals Posthumus to be still obsessed with
judgment. He has achieved forgiveness toward Imogen by turning the judgmental impulse upon himself—"Me, wretch, more
worth your vengeance" (5.1.11). His life to him is "every breath
a death" (5.1.27). He flings himself into battle, but soon com-
plains he "could not find death where I did hear him groan"
(5.3.69). He leaves off fighting to seek death unequivocally:

> For me, my ransom's death.
> On either side I come to spend my breath;
> Which neither here I'll keep nor bear again,
> But end it by some means for Imogen.
> (5.3.80–83)

Although he adopts a sacrificial tone, Posthumus' dedication to death evinces profound soul-sickness.

The burden of Posthumus' experiences in act 5 is to carry him from a legalistic view of sin, whereby death can be the only adequate payment for his crime, to an acceptance of grace, which demands an act of self-forgiveness. Posthumus' accusations against himself illustrate that an obsession with judgment is dangerous in private as well as in public contexts. He comes to recognize the inappropriateness of merely passing judgment, even on himself. The lesson is analogous to that in the Epistle appointed for the third Sunday in Advent: "I judge not mine own self" (*BCP* 81). But not until he discovers his identity, as family member and as fallible man, can Posthumus release himself from the quest for an absolute standard of behavior. His dream vision provides the means toward the change of heart.

Posthumus' imprisonment in 5.4, however it is represented on stage, manifests the emotional isolation that began for him in 1.2, when he departed from Imogen, and that has now deepened into a longing for death. Having lost his wife, his allegiance to the British throne, and his fighting spirit, Posthumus drops to the nadir of his fortunes. Although his prison meditation on "th' sure physician, death" (5.4.7) traces the three steps in repentance—attrition, penance, satisfaction (Skura, "Interpreting" 210)—his insistence that the gods take his life in payment for Imogen's is extravagent and imperious. Legal and mercenary images reveal him still obsessed with issues of judgment:

> Take
> No stricter render of me than my all.
> (5.4.16–17)

> 'Tween man and man they weigh not every stamp.
> (5.4.24)

> If you will take this audit, take this life,
> And cancel these cold bonds.
> (5.4.27–28)

Convinced he has murdered his wife, Posthumus seeks death as an escape from his burdened conscience. He seems more desperate than contrite.

In the complexly resonant dream vision, Shakespeare manipulates genre (the hero's discovery of his origins) and stage convention (deus ex machina). Psychoanalytic critics have supplied considerable insight into the dream's familial matrix and the way its discovery heals Posthumus. Skura notes that the dream allows Posthumus to "[recognize] his past and therefore [recognize] himself" ("Interpreting" 212). The substance of his family's message is vital to Posthumus' rebirth; the ghosts from the past appear on stage to teach him self-forgiveness. The action of the play begins to move toward the final overturning of judgment by forgiveness.

Jupiter, supposedly the reigning god of the play, is presented in somewhat equivocal terms; despite his impressive descent "*in thunder and lightning, sitting upon an eagle*" (5.4.92sd), the spectacle contains indications of an era in eclipse. Posthumus' father and mother berate the god for the harsh measure meted out to their son. Sicilius says Jupiter should have protected the orphaned boy. Posthumus' misdeeds are declared by the ghosts to be Jupiter's fault:

> Why did you suffer Jachimo,
> Slight thing of Italy
> To taint his nobler heart and brain
> With needless jealousy.
> (5.4.63–66)

Self-proclaimed intercessors, the ghosts call on Jupiter to explain the way Posthumus has been treated:

> Then, Jupiter, thou king of gods,
> Why hast thou thus adjourn'd
> The graces for his merits due,
> Being all to dolors turn'd?
> (5.4.77–80)

When the beleagured god appears, "offend[ed]" by the "petty spirits" (5.4.93, 94) who accuse him, he offers a strangely elliptical defense: "Whom best I love, I cross; to make my gift, / The more delay'd, delighted" (5.4.101–2). Posthumus, says Jupiter, will be "happier much by his affliction made" (5.4.108). The god's message "is rather a simple-minded one," for "this Jupiter is the remembered God of childhood, who loves but punishes us for our own good" (Hunter 171, 172).

The pagan/primal god's notion of purposeful suffering anticipates the doctrine of *felix culpa*. The *felix culpa* scheme is feasible only when history operates according to a divine plan; it presupposes happy faith in an omnipotent deity. For a Christian audience, Jupiter's assertion of his own command, as pagan god, over Posthumus' life proleptically suggests the Christian idea of purposeful history; hence in a certain sense he predicts the coming of the new era. This suggestion of Jupiter as a dying god lingers at the close of the play, when the soothsayer recalls the vision first mentioned at 4.3.346–52, now "full accomplish'd":

> for the Roman eagle,
> From south to west on wing soaring aloft,
> Lessen'd herself, and in the beams o' th' sun
> So vanish'd.
> (5.5.470–73)

The soothsayer interprets the vision politically but, given the apocalyptic resonances of the final scene, the disappearance of the eagle—Jupiter's bird—into the western sun seems to signal a new sun/son in the east.

Jupiter is associated with Old Testament law as well as with the pagan era. Posthumus' family argues that a worthy man deserves better treatment from a just god:

> Since, Jupiter, our son is good,
> Take off his miseries
> (5.4.85–86)

They demand "the graces for his merits due" (5.4.79). Bullied and heckled as he is by Posthumus' family, this god's power is curiously circumscribed, as though to invalidate his ethos. Sicilius' first line

> No more, thou Thunder-master, show
> Thy spite on mortal flies
> (5.4.30–31)

is effectively a prediction as well as a demand.

Ultimately the ghosts' appeal for clemency has most important application with regard to Posthumus himself, for they teach him the grounds for charity. Considerable distance lies between his family's view that Posthumus has "done aught but well" (5.4.35) and an audience's much more critical assessment of his behavior. But the vision signifies Posthumus' discovery of a lost childhood. The dream experience affords him the unconditional, all-forgiving love of parent for child, which apparently he has not before experienced. His mother calls him "a thing of pity!" (5.4.47), drawing on the full resonance of the term to suggest generous, open-hearted empathy. It is precisely the lack of this capacity for understanding and forgiveness that has inspired Posthumus' vindictiveness toward Imogen and his subsequent rigid self-appraisal. When, in the dream, his parents identify him as worthy of their pity, Posthumus discovers the grounds for becoming a charitable person—he first learns to pity and forgive himself. The springs of empathy are uncovered when he learns how he "came crying 'mongst his foes" (5.4.46). Echoing Lear's "we came crying hither" (*Lr.* 4.6.178), the line suggests the same newly found understanding of the original frailty of the human condition, a frailty never completely outgrown.

The guilt and disenchantment that drove Posthumus toward death vanish in the wake of the dream. The prophecy baffles him, but wonderment mixes with an overwhelming sense of acceptance as he says of the inscribed tablets:

> Be what it is,
> The action of my life is like it, which
> I'll keep, if but for sympathy.
> (5.4.148–50)

Although the meaning of the passage slips away like a dream— in Dr. Johnson's phrase, "too thin to be easily caught" (8: 905)— Posthumus apparently means he will "keep" not only the tablet but his life, which only a few moments before he was eager to doff. There is a submerged echo of Hamlet's

> If it be now,'tis not to come; if
> it be not to come, it will be now; if it be not now,
> yet it will come—the readiness is all.
> (*Ham.* 5.2.220–22)

Posthumus arrives at a similar acceptance of his fate. The immediate entry of the Gaoler, asking "come, sir, are you ready for death?" (5.4.151) and Posthumus' joking responses show how far the dream has brought him. Previously he wished to die because he was unable to live. Now he can accept his fate, be it life—he has gained the equanimity of a charitable disposition— or death—he has received an assurance that familial bonds extend beyond the grave.

In contrast to the funeral in act 4, which proclaimed repeatedly that "all must . . . come to dust," Posthumus' dream counts, for him at least, as an indication of life after death. His "death has eyes in's head" (5.4.178), in the Gaoler's words. The dream is closely correlated with All Souls' Day, on which the Roman church recalled its dead. "The Reformation left the English Church without All Souls, but it was partially assimilated to All Saints, the day before, and popular customs surrounding the cult of the dead survived" (Bender 239). All Saints' itself was "the last special feast before . . . Advent, a season with which it came to have vital associations" (Bender 237). Having partially absorbed the traditions of pagan Halloween, All Souls' and All Saints' together provided a brief period during which the dead were believed to walk abroad. All Souls', accomplishing in memory a resurrection of the dead, provided a preview of the final reunion at the end of time. In his prison cell, Posthumus does more than simply remember his family. His vision conjures up their spirits so that the past becomes, in the world of the play, literally present; and they leave behind a literal token. The reunion with the dead, coupled in the dream with the descent of a god, suggests Judgment Day.

3

The final scene of *Cymbeline* features a stunning number of reversals. Imogen forgives Posthumus for doubting her, testing her, and plotting to kill her. Posthumus forgives Jachimo for deceiving him. Cymbeline forgives Belarius for kidnapping his two sons, and then decrees that "pardon's the word to all" (5.5.422). The vindictiveness that has characterized his kingdom disappears in the face of this pardoning spirit. The sheer magnitude of forgiveness—Cymbeline even offers tribute to his defeated foe—violates expectations created by the rest of the play. Critics have either applauded the last scene as a virtuous display of technical genius or shuddered that the plot is "wound up in the quickest and most perfunctory manner" (Grene 40).

Hence the connection with Christ's nativity provides an apparently necessary gloss on the scene. The generosity of spirit evinced at the play's end suggests a sudden surplus of grace in Cymbeline's world, as though the tremendous event in Bethlehem had produced a moral fallout that settles over the pagan earth. The Gaoler, whose occupation has often been read allegorically as a reminder of a world in bondage (Frye, *Perspective* 66), seems to sense this incipient grace when he wishes "we were all of one mind, and one mind good" (5.3.203–4).[5] Beside the structure of *Cymbeline* lies a corollary action, whereby the Holy Birth, by its very occurrence, changes the world, albeit without the world's knowledge. This general correlation between the play's tragicomic structure and the pattern of Christian history helps to explain the transformation that occurs in King Cymbeline's realm. Still, one is left wondering why redemption is not offered universally—the queen is unaffected by the descending grace, and so is Cloten. Why, if a new dispensation is to be assumed, must Posthumus, Jachimo, Guiderius, and Belarius be judged or threatened with judgment before pardon is extended? Why do a decisive battle and the descent of a god precede the final, momentous change? The features of the play's conclusion, considered singly, are unremarkable in Renaissance drama. Occurring together, however, theophany, battle, reunion, collective judgment, and final peace become profoundly suggestive, for they follow the pattern of events expected to take place on Judgment Day. Recognizing the scene's apocalyptic ramifications clarifies the relationship between *Cymbeline* and Christian history.

The decisive battle fought at the play's end carries overtones of Armaggedon. It clears the way for a millennial change: "Never was a war did cease / (Ere bloody hands were wash'd) with such a peace" (5.5.484–85). After the battle, those who have been presumed dead—Cymbeline's three children—are effectively resurrected and restored to life. A systematic ordering of uncertain futures takes place in a succession of revelations less "continuous" than "contiguous" (Uphaus 67). A series of individual conflicts comes to light, characters make their confessions, judg-

5. The remark may echo Acts 2.1 in the King James Version: "They were all with one accord in one place." The topos of unity achieved from diversity is that of Judgment Day.

ment is threatened but then overturned by pardon. The stunning pronouncement of peace at the very conclusion has apparently obscured the extent to which judgment fuels this final scene. In fact, the play's action reaches resolution in 5.5. as if before a high court of justice: judgment is declared on the queen, Jachimo, Posthumus, Guiderius, Cloten, Pisanio, Belarius. In some cases judgment is self-inflicted, and in some it is overturned, but the process of hearing evidence and passing sentence precedes the turn to peace and absolution at the very last.

Divine judgment was understood in the Renaissance to occur in successive stages. John Donne spoke of three judgments: the first, before the creation, of "our Election"; next, that of "our Justification here"; finally, at Doomsday, that of "our Glorification, severing sheep from goats" (*Sermons* 2: 323). Jeremy Taylor spoke explicitly in an Advent sermon of the relationship between earthly and final judgments. Earthly law and the general "order of things" worked to uphold the essential distinction between virtue and vice. "But it is not enough that all the world hath armed itself against vice" because clandestine acts escaped notice. One purpose of Doomsday, therefore, was "that the private should be judged." More generally, the Last Judgment would correct mistaken earthly judgments:

> The cause that was ill-judged should be judged over again, and tyrants should be called to account, and our thoughts should be examined, and our secret actions viewed on all sides, and the infinite number of sins which escape here should not escape finally. ("Advent" 1–2)

In essence, then, the Last Judgment would dissolve all private judgments by bringing them into the public—the universal—arena.

An acknowledged duality between private and public actions can help explain Posthumus' behavior in the final scene. The equanimity instilled earlier in the play by his dream vision evaporates when Posthumus is confronted by Jachimo and Cymbeline. Despite Jachimo's admission of blame, Posthumus launches into a frenzy of self-incrimination:

> O, give me cord, or knife, or poison,
> Some upright justicer! Thou, King, send out
> For torturers ingenious; it is I
> That all th' abhorred things o' th' earth amend
> By being worse than they.
>
> (5.5.213–17)

His frustrations are reminiscent of his mood before the dream. As Kastan comments, "old habits of mind die slowly" (151). But the earlier change of heart is not necessarily invalidated. We are confronted here with one of the play's many conflicts between "inner" and "outer."[6] Although the theater audience is privileged to observe it, Posthumus' dream is an intensely private experience—he glimpses a lost childhood. The dream offers a balm that partially heals Posthumus' guilty death wish, but he still requires a public experience of rebirth. Putting it another way, one could say that Posthumus has been reconciled with one family, who exist only inside his memory, and now must seek reconciliation with his second family, who exist in the public arena. His words upon embracing Imogen—"hang there like fruit, my soul, / Till the tree die!" (5.5.263–64)—with their combined resonances of fertility, crucifixion, and marital imagery, constitute one of the most profound reunions in the last plays. Not the least of its effect lies in the challenge offered the audience to join the community onstage in also forgiving Posthumus (see Hunter 245).

Because Judgment Day was understood as a universal summary, the public response to a series of actions many of which had already been judged, even the queen and Cloten have their lives reviewed in the final scene. Having died in the course of the play, they are not here resurrected to receive judgment; they are physically excluded, as though the sheep have already been separated from the goats. Almost all Protestant theologians in the Renaissance affirmed the immediacy with which judgment followed death. William Perkins, for instance, wrote:

> When men die in the faith, their soules are immediately translated into heaven, and their [sic] abide till the last judgement: and contrariwise if men die in their sinnes,

---

6. Peterson comments on this duality with regard to the king: "The consequences of Cymbeline's folly are both 'public' and 'private' " (116).

their soules goe straight to the place of eternall condemnation and there abide as in a prison, as Peter saith. In a
word, when the breath goeth out of the bodie, the soule of
everyman goeth straight either to heaven or hell; and there
is no third place of aboad mentioned in Scripture.[7] ("Exposition" 324)

This insistence on immediate damnation or justification was
meant to counter various heresies, most importantly of course,
that of Purgatory, the "third place of aboad." But one conse-
quence of placing the crucial judgment at the moment of death
was the effectual emptying of purpose from Judgment Day. It
became the ritual reenactment of a division that had already been
made (Ariés 106–7, 153).

Hence the perfunctory quality of many of the judgments pro-
nounced in the final scene of *Cymbeline* accords with contemporary understanding of the Last Judgment: everyone must be
judged, but the judgments are in most cases predetermined.
So, for instance, the recitation of the queen's confessed crimes
suggests a life being summarized rather than weighed in the
balance. The distinctly Christian terms in which her death is
recounted are surprising, given her overwhelming resemblance
to the witch of a fairy tale. She "repented" (5.5.59)—albeit per-
versely, for she regretted unaccomplished murders, not her
sins—and "so / Despairing died" (5.5.60–61). Cymbeline dismisses the queen's account by pronouncing her the recipient of
divine justice:

> Our wicked queen,
> Whom heavens, in justice both on her and hers,
> Have laid most heavy hand.
> (5.5.463–65)

Cloten, somewhat similarly, is recalled in the final scene so
that his account can be set in order. Pisanio tells the sordid tale
of Cloten's violent pursuit of Imogen. Cymbeline's defense of
title—"he was a prince" (5.5.291)—is challenged by Guiderius'
defiant response—"a most incivil one," "nothing prince-like"
(5.5.292,293). The clashing of value systems is part of the larger

---

7. Other examples include John Woolton's *A Treatise of the Immortalitie
of the Soule* (93v) and Thomas Becon's *The Sicke Mans Salve* (322).

action of the scene (and the play), whereby inner virtues like charity displace outer ones like rank and authority. Guiderius, eventually forgiven by Cymbeline precisely because of his own princely rank, is correct in his assessment of Cloten, as well as generally triumphant in his ability to combine virtue with title.

Of those actually present in the final scene, Jachimo carries the heaviest load of guilt. Perhaps his admission to the community here owes to his early repentance. As early as 5.2.1–2 he has acknowledged "the heaviness and guilt within [his] bosom." "Iachimo is capable of the first essential step toward regeneration and, as a result, he can participate in the play's happy ending" (Hunter 175). In 5.5 he speaks of the "villainy" which it "torments [him] to conceal" (142), and kneels with "heavy conscience" (413) to offer his life to Posthumus. Posthumus' two contrasting responses to Jachimo in this scene illustrate the infectious power of forgiveness. Before his reunion with Imogen, Posthumus, sunk in his own guilt, calls Jachimo "Italian fiend!" (5.5.210), echoing Othello searching for Iago's cloven feet. After receiving the play's hardest lesson in forgiveness, however, Posthumus overturns his anger and everyone's expectations:

> Kneel not to me.
> The pow'r that I have on you is to spare you;
> The malice towards you, to forgive you. Live,
> And deal with others better.
>
> (5.5.417–20)

Posthumus finally frees himself from vengeance when he releases Jachimo from his guilty debt. It is the culmination of Posthumus' education in forgiveness, the sequence that illustrates the Advent theme of the arrival of a new dispensation of mercy.

The relationship between mercy and the law is at issue in the other two judgments at the close of the play, those of Guiderius and Belarius. Both have broken the law of the kingdom: Guiderius in beheading Cloten, Belarius in kidnapping Cymbeline's sons. Both believe their actions served justifiable purposes. In both cases, the law's significance crumbles when the happy results of Belarius' crime come to light. Intentions, inner laws, are shown to matter. Moreover, the moral and intellectual confusion engendered by passing events is dispersed when the outcome of every action becomes clear. One of the Advent readings advised,

"Judge nothing before the time . . . which will lighten things that are hid in darkness" (*BCP* 81). In any play, but especially in this play, that "time" is analogous to the final scene.

The law of Cymbeline's kingdom is overturned by generosity of spirit. The king's own vindictive impulse—he says "the whole world shall not save" Belarius (5.5.321)—disappears with the sudden access of joy at discovering his sons; he then accepts Belarius as "brother" (5.5.399). Cymbeline applauds Posthumus' decision to forgive Jachimo with a significant phrase—"nobly doom'd!" (5.5.420)—and himself completes the chain of forgiveness by announcing that "pardon's the word to all" (5.5.422). Cymbeline's personal decision to embrace forgiveness constitutes the scene's largest act of judgment, since it determines the course of his kingdom. When the regent "dooms" in favor of peace, he, in effect, transforms his realm from one of malice to one given over to celebration of good will. Yet the peaceful chord that closes the scene does not invalidate the dominant motif of judgment; instead, peace is the happy result of a "noble doom." The monarch resolves the conflict between judgment and forgiveness by uniting the two forces in one action.

4

In showing *Cymbeline* to be an apocalyptic play, I have concentrated primarily on the fearful aspects of the expected last day, as the Anglican Church did during Advent. Its dominant penitential tone, however, did not completely mute Advent's expectant and celebratory chords. And accordingly, the last scene of *Cymbeline* appeals to joyful, as well as fearful, anticipations of the last day. The scene occasions a grand reunion. This "soft" image of Judgment Day seems to have had wide currency in the Renaissance, even though it was not officially endorsed by either Roman or Anglican Church. George Herbert, for instance, in his poem "Doomsday" (one of five eschatological poems that close the central section of *The Temple*), pictures the general resurrection as a reunion in which "this member jogs the other, / Each one whispering, *Live you brother?*" (190). The jolly confusion of this imagined recognition markedly contrasts "that strange confusion" Donne preached of, which "shall overtake, and oppresse those infinite multitudes of Soules, which . . . shall receive an irrevocable judgment of everlasting condemnation" (*Ser*-

mons 5: 106). The Church employed images of Judgment Day for didactic purposes, as stated by Perkins:

> If we beleeve that our bodies shall rise againe after this life, and stand before God at the last day of judgement, we must daily enter into a serious consideration of this time, and have in minde, that one day we must meete the Lord face to face. ("Exposition" 323)

The Doomsday paintings so prevalent in English churches reinforced the terror of judgment, and although they were supposedly obliterated with the Reformation, Puritan complaints that "iconoclasm was half-hearted and whitewash insufficient" (Lascelles 75) suggest the continued visual presence of the panoramas of doom. In *Cymbeline*, the fearful spectre of the Apocalypse is reflected in the emphasis on physical death; it also influences the transformation of Posthumus' attitudes toward himself and others. In the final scene, however, these fearful attitudes toward the Last Day are largely absent. The dominant emotions of the last scene are wonder and surprise, not fear and trembling.

Conceptions of death and apocalypse underwent a number of striking changes in the medieval and Renaissance periods. Medieval Europe's earliest representations of the Apocalypse present majestic visions of the Second Coming, void of anything fearful. No firm geography of the afterlife yet existed—dead souls were pictured in Abraham's bosom.[8] In the twelfth and thirteenth centuries, an iconography of judgment gradually took hold, with images such as the court of justice and the weighing of souls provoking, as well as expressing, anxiety. The Doomsday plays in the mystery cycles reflect this medieval terror of the Apocalypse (see appendix A). The message—"repent before it is too late"—was emblematized by the final disappearance of the

8. The image of Abraham's bosom was resilient nevertheless: not only does the Hostess, notoriously, report Falstaff gone to "Arthur's boson" (*H5* 3.3.9), but Jeremy Taylor, preaching in 1657, distinguishes paradise from the bosom of Abraham: "To be with Abraham, or to sit down with Abraham, in the time of the Old Testament, did signify the same thing as to be in paradise; but to be in 'Abraham's bosom,' signifies a great eminence of place and comfort, which is indulged to the most excellent and the most afflicted" ("Funeral Sermon" 551).

damned into Hell Mouth. Because of the ultimate decisiveness of Judgment Day in this eschatology, the moment of individual death was relatively unimportant. Ariés writes of "the tame death," an apparently calm and unquestioning acceptance of mortality (128–29, 138–39, 604–6).

In the later Middle Ages, the decisive judgmental event was moved backward from the end of time to the moment of individual expiration. The concept of immediate judgment became crucial during the Reformation, when Protestants insisted that "the faithfull soule when it departeth out of this life is immediately after death with Christ" (Estwick 17). Immediate judgment was necessary in order to counter the doctrine of purgatory and the various heresies that sprang up with the abolition of "the third place." Increased focus on the moment of individual death emptied the general judgment of much of its terror, even as the Church continued to endorse the imminence of Judgment Day. As a result, by the early seventeenth century, Judgment Day was becoming a symbolic rather than a literal notion. D. P. Walker, who sees the softening of the Apocalypse as beginning much earlier, links the draining of terror to the delayed arrival of the Parousia:

> When the Second Coming receded into a remote future, there was a natural wish not to postpone indefinitely the reward of the saved and the punishment of the damned; hence the doctrine of the immediate judgment of each soul at death. But, since the Second Coming could not be entirely eliminated, the Last Judgement still remained, by now a superfluous ceremony for all but the tiny minority of men alive at the Last Day. (35)

Judgment Day, for some at least, took on aspects of an enormous family reunion, a day on which the living and the dead would once more be together. It became a focus for sentimental longings.

But concomitant with the growing idea of reunion after death was an increased horror of death itself. Not only did the moment of expiration matter terribly, since even a good person had much to fear from dying without spiritual preparation (like Hamlet's father, "grossly, full of bread, / With all his crimes broad blown" [*Ham.* 3.3.80–81]), but awareness of the precariousness of existence was exacerbated by growing humanistic valuation of this world's things and its people. Death became more emphatically the enemy. By postulating a personally appealing afterlife, one stood to recover, in effect, some of what death threatened to take away.

In Shakespeare's day, death was thought of as "the separation of the Soule from the bodie" (Mornay 240), or the unraveling of, as Donne put it, "that subtile knot, which makes us man" ("Exstasie" 61). The notion of separation encompasses its opposite, the corollary idea of reunion. The Church taught that on Judgment Day body and soul would come together again. The projected healing of severed body and soul made it possible to suppose that other severances caused by death—those between family and friends—might also be healed on the last day. The concept of reunion after death is a logical extension of that of bodily resurrection. The fairly heated debate waged in the early seventeenth century on the subjects of resurrection and reunion bears importantly on the restorations of severed relationships in each of Shakespeare's last plays, and I will discuss it more fully in the next chapter. Especially in *The Winter's Tale*, the topos of separation and reunion of husband and wife serves as a figure for restoration of the *homo totus*.

Cymbeline, a play deeply concerned with the relationships— Geller's "covenants"—connecting people with one another, closes with a vision of the social aspects of Judgment Day. In contrast to the other last plays, in which the lost are restored singly, *Cymbeline* features a vast reunion, in which almost everyone experiences the return of a loved one believed to be dead. Belarius, Arviragus, and Guiderius are baffled by the presence of "Fidele," the boy they have interred. Belarius' stunned question, "Is not this boy reviv'd from death?" (5.5.119), implies the possibility of resurrection, although he hesitates to assume this has happened. Guiderius, insisting "we saw him dead" (5.5.126), apparently thinks he sees "Fidele's" ghost before him. Pisanio, who has feared for Imogen's life, recognizes her in disguise. Posthumus discovers the wife he thinks he has killed. And Cymbeline's three children—the two sons missing some twenty years, the daughter presumed dead after her flight from court— are restored to him. Each individual discovery signals a reprieve from death; occurring together, the various recoveries suggest a collective deliverance. Those recovered are not ghosts like the spirits who appear in Posthumus' dream. The contrast underscores the ability of these restorations to suggest a permanent family reunion to occur at the end of time. The vision is all the more pointed for the absence of the queen and Cloten who remain dead, evidently dismissed to damnation. For the characters who experience the momentous revelations of the final scene, the future is utterly transformed, remade into a dream of all that death had denied them.

The play's keen attention to the physical fact of death, coupled with the glorious reunions at the play's close, betray an emotional drive to deny death's mastery. The action of *Cymbeline* illustrates the inescapability of death. The despairing queen dies unrepentant; Cloten is beheaded; Imogen lies comatose through a mock funeral. The confusion of Cloten's corpse with Posthumus' underscores the ontological sense of death. Cloten's body is, after all, only a body; it might as well be Posthumus'. Dying is shown to be a grotesque denial of human identity, but the play leaps at the last from this inevitable personal loss to the wondrous possibility of general reunion.

3
Reunion in The Winter's Tale

Not like a corse; or if—not to be buried,
But quick and in mine arms.
—The Winter's Tale

Earlier Shakespearean plays, notably *Much Ado About Nothing* and *1 Henry IV*, feature sudden revivals of characters believed to be dead. However, the motif reaches its fulfillment in the romances. Reunions with characters believed to be dead figure significantly in *Pericles, Cymbeline, The Winter's Tale,* and with slightly muted emphasis in *The Tempest.* Such unexpected returns are of course characteristic of romance as a genre, and in a formalist sense, one might say that any author is a god capable of killing and resurrecting his or her creatures at will. In drama, however, the physical component of a reunion receives crucial emphasis, since drama is an art of bodies as well as of words.

The Shakespearean motif of dramatic resurrection has attracted an enormous amount of critical attention, most of it discovering symbolic patterns, some of it finding recourse to religious terminology, but none of it, curiously, focusing on seventeenth-century discussions of bodily resurrection and reunion. Examining the particular historical contexts of Renaissance eschatology suggests that these returns, far from being the senile delusions of an old playwright, encompass a complex network of popular expectation. Shakespeare, moreover, exploits the physicality of his dramatic medium to emphasize the priority of bodies in what amounts to a proleptic vision of heaven. The physical emphasis of these reunions counters two parallel kinds of dualistic thought that together largely determine the orthodox Christian view of afterlife: the division of body from soul and the division of self from society. Shakespeare's reunion scenes base the existence of community upon the body. The image of fulfillment in the romances is one of restored human attachments.

1

Cymbeline twice reunites Imogen and Posthumus. The first reunion is the grotesque parody in which Imogen mistakenly embraces Cloten's corpse, and grieves for Posthumus. The second reunion, their public embrace in the play's last scene, fulfills the false copy, for until this crowded scene, each believes the other spouse dead. The public reunion corrects the scene in the burial plot most obviously by substituting Posthumus for Cloten, and even more fundamentally by providing a live body in place of a dead one. Imogen and Posthumus each undergo a type of death in the course of the action. Imogen is buried comatose; Posthumus endures a spiritual death reflected in the beheading of his double, Cloten. Their final reunion therefore suggests a meeting in the afterlife. The fortunate conclusion strongly contrasts the hollow embrace in the tomb, but the scenes share a distinctive physical concern:

> *Imogen.* Why did you throw your wedded lady from you?
>   Think that you are upon a rock, and now
>   Throw me again. *Embracing him.*
> *Posthumus:*   Hang there like fruit, my soul,
>   Till the tree die!
>   (*Cym.* 5.5.261–64)

Their embrace literally reconstitutes the marriage, with metaphor paradoxically managing to solidify spiritual reunion. Their marriage is a rock founded on Imogen's body (or, in alternative texts, a "lock," fastening the couple together); Posthumus' soul hangs heavy as "fruit." The insistence on physicality undermines any temptation to understand their reunion as the spiritual fulfillment of Imogen's previous mistake. Although it is an embrace of souls, the spiritual reunion is "fruit[ful]" and, moreover, absolutely predicated upon the physical embrace. Cymbeline breaks in with words that emphasize the point: "How now, my flesh? My child?" (5.5.264).

Pericles, similarly, must touch his child's flesh before he is able to recognize her:

> Didst thou not say, when I did push thee back—
> Which was when I perceiv'd thee—that thou cam'st
> From good descending?
>   (*Per.* 5.1.126–28)

Pericles, nearly catatonic when Marina first approaches, alarms some critics with his sudden roughness. The incest threat hanging over the relationship may be momentarily manifested in this "push." Yet the action's primary importance is that it forces open Pericles' memory of his dead wife and daughter. He must resurrect this memory before he can recognize Marina, and yet, paradoxically, Marina must be resurrected for him—he must touch her—before he can discover the image. The moment when Pericles pushes Marina is crucial; neither her singing, nor her recited genealogy, nor her resemblance to Thaisa would count for anything without the initial physical breakthrough.

The Winter's Tale features the most emphatic instance of physical reunion, for initially it seems that Leontes has been given *only* Hermione's body, or something indistinguishable from it. The device of the statue isolates and intensifies a concern with the physical self that characterizes the reunions with Imogen, Thaisa, Marina, and Hermione. Through the long passage during which Hermione remains on the pedestal, the audience shares Leontes' acute, even uncomfortable, awareness of the merging parameters of art, life, and death. Can the statue bear every appearance of Hermione and not be the queen herself? The suspense continues even when she steps down and embraces her husband, even when he gasps, "O, she's warm!" (5.3.109), for the court party demands that Hermione speak before they accept her as living, and Paulina's engimatic "it appears she lives" (5.3.117) raises more questions than it answers. Hermione's omission of any address to Leontes, troubling though it may be, trains the dramatic focus relentlessly on her physical presence, which alone can distinguish this reunion from dream, or memory, or spiritual communion with the dead (all of which occur elsewhere in the play). Hermione's living body is given back to Leontes after she has been, the play all but insists, dead.

Each of the recoveries in Shakespeare's last plays involves two steps: rescue from near or apparent death and reunion with others. In every case but Hermione's, the two steps occur separately; and the audience is privy to the escape of Marina, the healing of Thaisa, the awakening of Imogen, the preservation of Ferdinand, and the rescue of Perdita. Only in the statue scene does Shakespeare show simultaneously the restoration of the body and the restoration of the family. Theatrically, the merging of procedures is a device designed to catch the audience off guard. One of its concomitant effects is to foreground the body. The audience may leave the theater still moved by Hermione's physical reappearance, not yet sufficiently distanced to insert the event into the play's design. By way of contrast, Thaisa's recovery, also miraculous, occurs early enough in *Pericles* that the audience adjusts to it long before the final reunion scene. Hermione's statue functions as a conduit for audience (and critical) attention; in doing so, it graphically illustrates the importance of the body to the fulfillment of desires. "What individuals share most vitally in common is the body: it is by virtue of our bodies that we belong to each other," writes Terry Eagleton (43). The various materialisms informing the assumptions of much contemporary criticism have lately encouraged attention to the physical dimensions of an author's vision. And while some such physical grounding is self-evidently a part of drama, the issue falls into particularly complex designs when a dramatic resurrection is at stake.[1]

Because of the ambiguity on stage between the representation of live and dead bodies, both ordinarily enacted by living actors, the audience depends on the responses of Leontes and Perdita in determining that the statue is, in fact, Hermione. She achieves a living identity, the sort of spiritual existence that distinguishes live bodies from statues and corpses, through the responses of those around her. Operation of the coup de theatre thus involves an audience's recognition that life inheres in communal bonds and emotional ties. Restoration of community is a central theme in the play. Animation of a statue kept "lonely, apart" (5.3.18) could only mock the woman who was Hermione.

The return of Hermione is at once far more concrete than the "symbolic rebirth" theory would have it and far less mundane than appeals to Paulina's household can suggest. Criticism of *The Winter's Tale* is divided between approaches that discover miraculous or transcendent elements and those that insist on seeing the action as naturalistic. Brian Cosgrove suggests that the critical split might be encompassed by defining "cyclical rebirth" as "an analogy of redemption from death." He sees in the

---

1. I have discussed some of these ideas with reference to changing customs in seventeenth-century tombstone monuments in "Dualism and the Hope of Reunion in *The Winter's Tale*," *Soundings* 69.3 (1986): 294–309.

play "an attempt to present, within the secular limits of drama, certain truths which we should usually think of as Christian" (181). Cosgrove usefully points to the analogies between religious and naturalistic approaches to the play, but the question of the drama's relation to the truths presumed to be outside the theater needs further examination. What are the implications of secularizing Christian notions of rebirth, if indeed that is Shakespeare's task?

Dennis Bartholomeusz, writing on *The Winter's Tale*, asserts that Shakespeare "enjoy[ed] playing off his own sense of resurrection in life, against the more traditional idea of resurrection after death, a great Elizabethan commonplace" (27). I think Bartholomeusz is right to recognize that Shakespeare somehow counters Christian tradition, although the notion of "resurrection in life" seems to imply symbolic renewal, and hence to allegorize the reunion. The intense physicality of Hermione's return is belied by such a reading. Furthermore, the play presents the return as a miraculous action, quite different from the more ordinary experience of life's fresh starts. Hermione's return is not for Leontes merely a symbol of his own rebirth, and it seems doubtful that the statue's descent would have had a primarily figurative meaning to a Jacobean audience. What overwhelms Leontes, and still overwhelms theater audiences, is the physical reunion with this particular woman who was dead.

It is useful to recognize that Hermione's return recalls a tradition of dramatized resurrection. (See appendix B, "*The Winter's Tale* and the Corpus Christi Resurrection Plays.") Secularization of the medieval resurrection plays provides much of the dramatic power of Hermione's return. But this reunion, and to an extent all those in the last plays, specifically and even radically counter Christian tradition. Against the scriptural assertion that "in the resurrection they nether marie wives, nor wives are bestowed in mariage, but are as the Angels of God in heaven" (Matt. 22.30), Shakespeare offers an ideal ending—theater's eschatology—that restores human attachments.

Living in a world of physical forms, we recognize others, even those we know most intimately (and, we suppose, spiritually) by their bodies. The reconstituted families in the romances image an intrinsic human hope of being given back our bodies, and hence each other, after death. It is precisely the wish for reunion that causes the souls in Dante's *Paradiso* to long for their bodies:

> They plainly
> showed their desire for their dead bodies,—not
> perhaps for themselves alone, but for their mothers,
> for their fathers, and for the others who were dear
> before they became eternal flames.
>
> (3.14.61–65)

Dante writes of the desire for physical restitution; Shakespeare's romances achieve a further point by dramatizing physical reunion.

2

Shakespeare's first dramatized resurrection, that of Falstaff in *1 Henry IV*, neatly summarizes certain issues which figure importantly in the romances. As Falstaff lies with Hotspur "in blood" (5.4.110), the two fallen characters an emblem of the ambiguous relation between live actors and dead characters, Prince Henry delivers two eulogies, evincing two fundamentally different attitudes toward death. Orthodox Anglican church officials would approve of the Prince's dualistic—indeed, fairly commonplace—eulogy for Hotspur:

> Ill-weav'd ambition, how much art thou shrunk!
> When that this body did contain a spirit,
> A kingdom for it was too small a bound,
> But now two paces of the vilest earth
> Is room enough.
>
> (5.4.88–92)

Praise follows the still-ambitious spirit "to heaven" (5.4.99), while Percy's "ignominy" will "sleep with [him] in the grave" (5.4.100). The balance is perfectly rendered, like that in Ben Jonson's "On My First Daughter," in which the child's soul is imagined in heaven and, "while that sever'd doth remaine, / This grave partakes the fleshly birth" (12). The Anglican burial service illustrates this sort of body-soul dualism in its instruction to mourners to rejoice for the departed soul, now "delivered from the burden of the flesh" (*BCP* 312).

Certainly Henry understands Falstaff's flesh to be a burden: "could not all this flesh / Keep in a little life?" (*1H4* 5.4.102–3). His condemnation of Falstaff's corpulence and cowardice deepens the antithesis between "flesh" and "life" in the direction of Manichaeism. Yet Henry's formulation collapses when *"Fal-*

43

staff riseth up" (5.4.110sd). The body-soul distinction becomes suddenly useless to the audience; Falstaff is reinstated in the action because his body, not his soul, has risen. Falstaff, "so grossly material that he can hardly move" (Eagleton 15), in fact *is* his body, in a way that Hotspur is not. Even if he eventually dies babbling of the "green fields" of heaven (*H5* 2.3.17), Falstaff's own understanding of human existence is distinctly materialistic:

> To die is to be a
> counterfeit, for he is but the counterfeit of a man who
> hath not the life of a man.
> (*1H4* 5.4.115–17)

An idealist, even a foolish idealist like Hotspur, fits nicely with Christian tradition; his final escape from the dross of earthly existence fulfills his desired "leap" toward "honor" (*1H4* 1.3.201–2). Falstaff, however, resists separation into component parts of body and soul, rising up in *1 Henry IV* from the guise of death to belie such a formulation. His return predicts those in the last plays because, for one thing, the audience's emotional attachment to him helps fuel the resurrection and, for another, it is difficult to conceive of his existence apart from his body. Goldman writes: "His appeal is so physical that it takes on the disarming clarity of an idea" (7). Falstaff stands unique among those "resurrected" in the Shakespearean canon, in not existing in a relationship of spouse or child. Shakespeare chooses, with good reason, to restore those who command most emotional attention. Moreover, since relationships with spouses and children involve obviously physical ties, restoration of these particular attachments further emphasizes the role of the body in reunion.

The concept of resurrection acknowledges in itself a human love for the body. The Anglican burial service includes a reading from Job 19 that promises restitution of the *homo totus*:

> I know that my redeemer liveth, and that I shall rise out of the earth in the last day, and shall be covered again with my skin, and shall see God in my flesh: yea, and I myself shall behold him, not with other, but with these same eyes.
> (*BCP* 309)

Christianity, inheriting and affirming this ancient Hebraic concept of human wholeness, was "not purely, or even primarily, dualistic," in the words of Jeffrey Russell. Yet Christian tradition received the effects of dualistic thinking from two sources:

> First, Jesus and the primitive Christian community were influenced by the teachings of the Essenes, who in turn had come under the influence of Persian dualism. Second, as Christianity became progressively hellenized, Greek philosophical dualism made a deep and durable mark upon it. (Russell 189)

In large part through the Neoplatonic sympathies of St. Augustine, Christian mortality came eventually to be characterized by extreme dualism, such as that expressed by St. Ambrose:

> Our soul is not buried with our body in the tomb. . . . It is pure waste that men build sumptuous tombs as though they were receptacles [*receptacula*] of the soul and not merely of the body. . . . The dwelling place of the soul is on high. (LeGoff 32–33)

In this formulation, the body is mere dross to be cast off; the soul, the important component of the "self," lives on. At its Platonized extreme, the notion of spiritual immortality makes resurrection of the body unnecessary (Cullmann 19).

One force behind the Reformation was a reaffirmation of materialism: "Protestants broke fundamentally with the subordination of nature to grace, secular to religious pursuits, and temporal to spiritual ends that had characterized the majority medieval traditon," writes Stephen Ozment (118). Luther directed attention back to resurrection, asserting that Christ's rising from the dead "is the chief article of the Christian doctrine" (28: 94). The desire to save the body from oblivion is expressed by John Woolton, Bishop of Exeter, who wrote in 1576 that if the "whole man consisting of body & soule, was fashioned after the Image & likenes of God," it followed that the "whole man" should enter the afterlife. Further, "the body so divinely united unto the soule, and indeed with such notable ornamentes, is not to be defrauded of that which of right ought to be yeelded unto it" (*Anatomie* 10r). John Donne similarly maintained that "all that is falne, receives a resurrection . . . the person, the whole man, not taken in pieces, soule alone, or body alone, but both" (*Sermons* 7: 103).

Christian eschatology has been disputed at all times and has usually been vaguely defined. Yet it is probably inevitable, given the early dualistic influences, that Christianity privilege a spiritual human component over a physical one. Particularly with regard to death, Christian consolation depends upon some degree of dualism. Because believers can see the body's fate all too clearly, consolation requires positing an existence that escapes corruption. The Anglican Church in Renaissance England made two promises regarding afterlife: immediate entry of the soul into the afterlife and eventual resurrection of the body. During the interval of separation, the disembodied soul would supposedly be happy (if it was in heaven), but not entirely happy, since it would miss the body. As seventeenth-century theologian Richard Baxter put it:

> The soul separated from the body, is not a perfect man, so it doth not enjoy the Glory and happiness so fully and so perfectly as it shall do after the Resurrection, when they are again conjoined. (279)

The relative degrees of heavenly bliss in Baxter's formulation signal an attempt to compensate for dualism in the afterlife. But Luther, characteristically asserting human wholeness, scoffed at the notion of a dualistic heaven: "That would be a silly soul if it were in heaven and desired its body!" (54: 447).

The Reformation in a sense upset a workable notion of individual fate after death. The concept of purgatory served the Roman Church well: it lessened death's finality by extending the period of trial and the possibility for redemption, and it provided a legitimate dwelling place for departed souls. Loss of the familiar tripartite geography of the afterlife produced anxiety. The projected interval between death and final resurrection in particular led some Protestants to speculation about ideas outside their doctrine, including the "third place" and the related notions of prayer for the dead and appeals to saints.

One fascinating response to anxieties about the afterlife was the heresy of mortalism, an idea strongly apposite to the emotions and the structure of *The Winter's Tale*. Mortalists denied the conscious existence of the human soul from the moment of death until the Last Judgment. Some believed that both body and soul die, and that both would be resurrected; others maintained that the soul was unconscious until Judgment Day. Unlike orthodox Christian eschatology, which assigned only the body to the grave, the heresy in effect extended the grasp of death. Mortalists accordingly placed supreme emphasis on resurrection as the act of new creation that would redeem both body and soul from death. Mortalists believed the notion of an immortal soul to be contrary to experience and to rational thought. It was more logical, they believed, to assume that both body and soul cease to exist, and that both body and soul will be resurrected. Instead of positing one component of human existence, the soul, to be virtually immune to death, mortalists applied Christianity's tragicomic pattern (death followed by resurrection) to each individual in two aspects, body and soul. Theirs was an extreme form of Christian faith in resurrection.

Mortalism at one time or another included among its adherents John Milton, Thomas Hobbes, and Sir Thomas Browne. But speculative theologians were by no means its only supporters; it had broad popular following (Burns 147). The heresy provided a logical defense against Roman Catholic notions of the afterlife. Yet it apparently appealed so widely because it answered another threat, less well defined but nonetheless of deep concern. The interval during which body and soul would be separated, according to orthodox doctrine, loomed as a profound threat to individual identity. Placing the soul alongside the body in the grave abolished, though at considerable cost, the spectre of a disembodied soul. It eliminated what Calvin called "that violent separation, which nature shunneth" (*On Genesis* 164; qtd. in Kerrigan 128).

Mortalism expresses the same swelling sense of individual integrity that caused rejection of the biblical precept "no mariage in heaven." In Renaissance England there was a drive to solidify heaven, to remake it in an earthly image. Mortalists could deny the existence of a disembodied soul during the interval between death and resurrection only by annihilating it or putting it to sleep. Others, heterodox rather than heretical, avoided the threat of disincarnate souls by importing bodies into their pictures of the ideal world. *The Winter's Tale* shares with mortalism a keen valuation of the body and a resultant emphasis on resurrection. Mortalism's balancing of rational experience with miracle bears a curious thematic appropriateness to *The Winter's Tale*, with its structural rhythm of loss and recovery, and mortalism can gloss the statue scene in subtle but powerfully suggestive ways. The play insists that Hermione is dead, then restores her to life by theatrical miracle. On stage, death implicates body and soul together, since no character can be separated from the actor's body, the moving statue that portrays him or her. Drama assumes a kind of mortalism, because it weighs the "body" and the "soul" of its characters equally.

3

Without bodies, human knowledge of the other is imperfect; and without others, we cannot perfectly know ourselves. Social relations are the medium in which we live our lives, and as such they do not simply reflect identity but constitute and define it. Eschatology, like drama, projects an arena in which the individual self meets, interacts, and merges with society. Eschatology attempts to connect the personal experience of death with a universal conception of ending. Prayers for the hastening of the kingdom, such as those found at the conclusion of the Elizabethan burial service (*BCP* 313), attest to this desire for heavenly society. But communal concerns are oddly absent from many orthodox Renaissance descriptions of heaven.

Renaissance theologians typically describe heaven by negation: the ideal is contrasted to the known world, and undesirable aspects of earthly reality are excised. Death, of course, would be no more; the blessed would be free

> from all defects and imperfections, diseases and distempers, infirmities and deformities, maimednesse and monstrous shapes, infancy, or decrepitnesse of stature, &c. [and] From want of meate, drinke, mariage. . . . (Bolton 129–30)

Despite the repeated caveat that our limited human perception can scarcely glimpse what will then be clear to a glorified understanding, descriptions such as Bolton's tend to labor under an awareness of their own insufficiency. Eliminating life's troubling experiences, they eliminate as well most everything that people ordinarily regard as making existence worthwhile. A note of compunction, even defensiveness, frequently accompanies the revelation that the superior delight of heaven would consist wholly in giving praise to God. George Gifford, for instance, in a sermon published in 1596, said:

> Partly through blindnes, wee see not how worthie hee [God] is of all glorie and praise: and partly through the remnants of corruption which remaine, wee have small delight to magnifie him, and we doe soone waxe wearie. But when we shall be made perfect like to the angels in heaven, than shall it bee otherwise with us. (368)

Human desires, in other words, will change, so that a heaven that seems unattractive to a fallen understanding would fulfill a glorified one. Theologians were bound to defend this militaristic heaven: John Woolton emphasizes the "willing obedience & service of god, with al our harts, with al our minds, with al our willes and with all our strength" that will characterize the "endles felicitie" (*Anatomie* 47r) of the godly. Descriptions such as these had political overtones, certainly; yet they purported to provide readers with a conception of afterlife.

Describing the future life was problematic long before the Renaissance. Biblical parables describe the "kingdom of heaven" allegorically by means of a mustard seed, a prodigal son, a wedding feast. Virtually the only gospel text that seems to address specific concerns about the afterlife in concrete terms is that proclaiming "no mariage in heaven." Appearing in two of the synoptic gospels, the passage inevitably attracted a great deal of interest in an age when divorce and afterlife were both hotly debated in England. During the Elizabethan and Jacobean eras, the passage from Luke was read each year at Morning Prayer on November 4—only a few days after All Saints' Day, with its lesson of imminent judgment and its careful regard for the dead. The question set to Jesus concerns a woman who has had seven husbands; the answer:

> The children of this worlde marie wives and are maried. But they which shalbe counted worthie to enjoy that worlde, and the resurrection from the dead, neither marie wives, nether are maried. For they can dye no more, forasmuche as they are equal unto the Angels. (Luke 20.34–36)

The text confirms that saints will not experience earthly desires. The exclusion of marriage, however, seems to exclude the possibility of reunion in heaven.

Some Renaissance theologians interpreted the passage by appealing to God's sense of biological necessity: reproduction will be unnecessary when death is no more. So John Woolton explained in his *Newe Anatomie of Whole Man,* "because there shalbe no mortality, mariage shall not be then needefull by new procreation, to preserve and continue natures and substances" (42v). As Luther perceived, the real point is that heaven will be utterly unlike temporal reality. "In short, all that pertains to the essence of these temporal goods and is part of temporal life and works will cease to be" (28: 172).

But the anxiety provoked by the idea of no marriage in heaven suggests the retrogressive habits of human desires. Many believers wished for a familiar heaven; heaven could be conceived as a reward only if it fulfilled the person and his or her wishes. The problem is essentially that of an afterlife based on a dualistic conception of the self. The orthodox Christian heaven is designed for the soul, which might be satisfied by spiritual communion with the saints. The body would enter heaven in a glorified state, but the desires we identify as bodily, including the desire for human relationships, are excluded. And as Shakespearean drama continually illustrates, these desires are as constitutive of the self as is spiritual awareness.

In an age when humanism, Protestantism, and the rising middle class were each contributing to enhanced valuation of marriage, permanent loss of human attachments seemed to some a high price for eternal bliss. John Donne pondered the passage on "no marriage in heaven" with a series of equivocable assertions:

> They shall not mary, because they shall have none of the uses of mariage. . . . But yet, though Christ exclude that, of which there is clearly no use in heaven, Mariage, (because they need no physick, no mutuall help, no supply of children) yet he excludes not our *knowing,* or our *loving* of *one another* upon former knowledge in this world, in the next; Christ does not say expressly we shall, yet neither does he say, that we shall not, *know one another* there. (*Sermons* 8:99)

Donne uneasily attempts to wrest his desired meaning from a textual lacuna ("yet neither does he say, that we shall not"). With a similar sort of ambivalence, William Perkins condemns the question about recognition in the afterlife as "ignorant," a typical concern of "them that have little religion in their hearts," and then proceeds to affirm "that men in heaven shal know each other: yea they shal know them which were never known or seene of them before in this life," although he hesitates over "whether they shall knowe one another after an earthly manner" ("Exposition" 326). The immensely popular Robert Bolton is freer in his logical construction. He thought that since heaven offers "every good thing," and meeting "our old deare Christian friends" pleases us, then "we shall know one another. Society is not comfortable, without familiar acquaintance" (145).

The seventeenth-century debate over human relationships in heaven ponders the questions of loss and restoration in a context relevant to Shakespeare's romances. Luther remarks that there is not "any death more bitter than that which separates a married couple. Only the death of children comes close to this; how much this hurts I have myself experienced" (54: 33). But the public statement of the Anglican church regarding emotional loss was far less candid. According to the "Exhortation on the Feare of Death," one of the homilies appointed by Queen Elizabeth to be read in churches, "men doe commonly feare death" for three reasons:

> First, the Sorrowful departing from worldly goods and plea-
> sures. The second, the feare of the pangs and paines that
> come with death. Last and principall cause is, the horrible
> feare of extreame misery, and perpetuall damnation in time
> to come. (*Certaine Sermons* 62)

The omission of any specific mention of sorrowful parting from loved ones is striking. The homily's consolation does not approach the pain of Lear's loss: "Thou'lt come no more, / Never, never, never, never, never" (5.3.308–9). Nor does it prepare for the wonder of Leontes' reunion with Hermione. The "Exhortation," the sort of official statement that exists primarily to placate anxieties, was careful to avoid issues for which the Church had no satisfactory answer. And recalcitrant emotional attachments clouded the orthodox picture of heaven.

The lines of the debate between those who insisted, with Woolton, that in heaven "there shall be no delight in carnal pleasure, in propagation of children, in mariages, in worldly regimentes" (*Anatomie* 47v) and those who maintained that though "death breakes off our societie, yet there shall be a day of meeting" (Adams 739) seem not to have been drawn on sectarian grounds. John Donne was high-church Anglican; Robert Bolton was a Puritan. Like many eschatological debates, the controversy intensified private concerns, sometimes with the result of wrenching individuals away from orthodox structures of belief. The debate over marriage in heaven demonstrates the general tension existing within a society focused on eschatological issues, but a society in which the Church's central authority was gradually eroding.

Shakespearean romance provided an image of marriage in heaven, for the theatrical reunions in the plays adumbrate the apocalyptic reunions offered more ambiguously by the Church. Romance is a genre of wish fulfillment. As such it tends to arise, writes Fredric Jameson, at particular moments of history. Romance "expresses a transitional moment," and "its contemporaries must feel their society torn between past and future" (158). Renaissance England experienced one such "transitional moment" with regard to its eschatology, when the medieval notion of afterlife as a spiritual reward began losing sway. This was just the beginning of the secularization of death and immortality.

4

Paulina's claim that Perdita's recovery

> Is all as monstrous to our human reason
> As my Antigonus to break his grave,
> And come again to me
> (5.1.41–43)

forecasts what it ostensibly denies—a resurrection from the dead. The remark joins the host of references in 5.1 to Hermione's "memory" (50), "her sainted spirit" (57), her "ghost" (63), "another, / As like Hermione as is her picture" (73–74), in creating a context for the queen's return. References to Hermione "again in breath" (83) predict the final scene. Hence they prepare Leontes, and the audience, for a wondrous possibility by creating a mental image of what will imminently occur on stage.

At the first glimpse of Hermione's statue, the audience may

momentarily wonder if a live actor or a cunning replica stands before them. Then follows the uncertainty as to whether the actor represents a thing of stone or a woman pretending to be stone. The audience is buffeted within the theatrical experience. At the same time they are struck by an awareness of the experience as theater. The moment is similar to that at the close of *King Lear* when, confronted by a body of indeterminate status, an audience may feel a brief upsurge of hope (perhaps Cordelia has survived), which is quickly dashed. Both scenes exploit the indeterminancy, on stage, between living and dead bodies to remind us of the inexact correspondence between a living person and his or her corpse. The realistic counterpart of this particular theatrical experience is that of confronting a dead body and feeling strangely baffled because the "person" is no longer in the corpse.

Christianity responds to this confusion by positing two selves, or parts of the self, only one of which dies ("When that this body did contain a spirit . . ." [*1H4* 5.4.89]). Yet much of human experience teaches that the body with its demands is the constitutive "self"—at least until the point of death, when the soul is said to become the surviving self. In Freud's analysis, the object of such dualism is to deny death, at whatever cost:

> It is true that the proposition "All men are mortal" is paraded in text-books of logic as an example of a generalization, but no human being really grasps it, and our unconscious has as little use now as ever for the idea of its own mortality. Religions continue to dispute the undeniable fact of the death of each one of us and to postulate a life after death. ("The Uncanny" 149)

These remarks occur in Freud's essay describing "The Uncanny," that feeling of creeping terror "which leads back to something long known to us, once very familiar" (123–24). The statue scene in *The Winter's Tale* encompasses several of the specific experiences Freud discusses: "intellectual uncertainty whether an object is alive or not," confusion related "to death and dead bodies, to the return of the dead, and to spirits and ghosts" (139, 149), and feelings of compulsive repetition, which Paulina incites by instructing Leontes,

> Do not shun her
> Until you see her die again, for then
> You kill her double.
>   (5.3.105–7).

Paulina attempts to stir Leontes' conscience—again—with the outrageous possibility that he might kill the queen twice over.

Paulina's words also suggest that the figure is actually not Hermione but "her double." This construction is strengthened by the previous references to Hermione's "ghost" and "spirit," and to "another, / As like Hermione as is her picture" (5.1.73–74). The possible fracturing of Hermione's identity fulfills another of Freud's circumstances that may create the experience of the uncanny. A dualistic concept of body and soul can be perverted into a fractured sense of self and double. Freud follows Otto Rank in his belief that the phenomenon of the double arises from an attempt to construct an assurance of immortality. Freud writes:

> The "double" was originally an insurance against destruction to the ego, an "energetic denial of the power of death," as Rank says; and probably the "immortal" soul was the first "double" of the body. . . . Such ideas . . . have sprung from the soil of unbounded self-love, from the primary narcissism which holds sway in the mind of the child as in that of primitive man; and when this stage has been left behind the double takes on a different aspect. From having been an assurance of immortality, he becomes the ghastly harbinger of death. ("The Uncanny" 141)

Hermione's animated statue figures most manifestly as "an assurance of immortality," defeating death (at least her death) in the play; but the statue derives an eerie power from its ability to play the double's opposite role as well. Stepping from its tomb, the dead-living statue is a "ghastly harbinger of death." The statue offers a similar sort of substitute immortality as the funeral effigy, an artifice that attempts to defy death by retaining an image of the body, but whose context—the funeral—acknowledges the ultimate power of destruction.

Another use of the doubling motif in *The Winter's Tale* enriches its importance in the statue scene. Leontes' jealousy can be traced to the doubling mechanism that identifies him with Polixenes. The idea is introduced in 1.2 when Polixenes, asked to describe himself and Leontes as boys, says,

> We were as twinn'd lambs that did frisk i' th' sun,
> And bleat the one at th' other. What we chang'd
> Was innocence for innocence.
>
> (1.2.67–69)

Frye suggests the words touch off a sense of suppressed guilt; some attribute to Leontes a repressed, or even manifest, homosexual anxiety ("Recognition" 192). Richard Begam believes the words signify the role of the double, a role Polixenes played for Leontes in childhood, serving to amplify the ego. But since the double must eventually be recognized as *other*, his separateness becomes a token of loss. Polixenes, by reminding Leontes of the union they originally shared, recalls to him also how the friends have since separated—reminds him of the loss incurred in investing oneself in another person, who will inevitably go away. The double, as mirror image of the self, is initially perceived as affirming one's immortality, but by ultimately affirming separability, suggests how the self may be fractured. When Leontes says to Hermione, "You have mistook, my lady, / Polixenes for Leontes" (2.1.81–82), he is himself confusing Polixenes' role with his own, interpolating his friend's presence into his own wife's bed. Leontes' banishing of friend, wife, counselor, and baby can be seen as the desperate maneuvers of an insecure personality to assert its power, to clear a place for itself in the world. But he succeeds instead in emptying his world of everything but his guilty conscience, personified in Paulina.

Only when Leontes receives a legitimate "assurance of immortality"—the return of his daughter—do his conflicts begin to be resolved. The play finally demands that Leontes "believe in the possibility of the other in the face of that most inescapable fact of human experience—death" (Begam 14). Hermione's sixteen-year absence confirms what Leontes could not initially appreciate—that she is truly separate, not a projection of his mind ("Your actions are my dreams" [3.2.82], he says in the trial scene), not the "twinn'd lamb" of childhood narcissism, and that the very fact of her otherness makes their bond a creative one. His wife is the other who can complete Leontes' self; he receives, in the last scene, stunning assurance that the loss sustained in loving another person will ultimately be made good.

The Winter's Tale is thus framed by the doubling motif. Polixenes, with whom Leontes identified himself in childhood, appears to him a haunting double in 1.2. Hermione figures as constructive double in the last scene. As the other who can affirm Leontes' self, and as the emblem of resurrection who affirms life after death—"bequeath[ing] to death [her] numbness" (5.3.102)—Hermione is, so to speak, doubly double. The play elaborates the motif on numerous levels: in the splintering of Leontes' narcissistic self, in the images of Hermione's spirit, in the statue initially offered as an alternative to Hermione. Hermione's restoration heals each cleavage of identity. Leontes becomes whole through their reconstituted marriage. When the statue speaks, demonstrating that this physical form is in fact Hermione, the play makes its case against body-soul dualism. At the same time, it acknowledges the importance of familial or communal restoration.

5

Psychoanalytic criticism illuminates the importance in Shakespeare's plays of, in Meredith Skura's words, "specific moments in . . . the cycle of generations that makes up a family" ("Interpreting" 204). The familial moment of death has peculiar importance, for it encompasses both absence and implied presence. Loss of child or spouse or parent unleashes a flood of emotions, including hope of eventual reunion. "The one unbearable dimension of possible human experience," writes Jacques Lacan, " is not the experience of one's own death, which no one has, but the experience of the death of another" (37). While threatened death of self implies destruction of the individual ego, death of the other threatens the obliteration as well of every bond, every shared hope, everything human experience can teach of love. When, in the romances, Shakespeare restores those who have been thought dead, he provides an image of hope which the Church largely declined to offer. The image is, however, self-consciously theatrical: when Paulina says "it appears [Hermione] lives," she points out that an audience can believe in events on stage, which are acknowledged to be appearances. Belief in religious promises is another matter altogether.

New Historicists have recently directed attention to the ways that deep-seated cultural upheaval in Renaissance England provided unique conditions under which the theater flourished. Drama, as Raymond Williams perceives, bears an inverse relation to cultural systems:

> What in the history of thought may be seen as a confusion or overlapping is often the precise moment of the dramatic impulse, since it is because the meaning and the experiences are uncertain and complex that the dramatic mode is more powerful. (72; qtd. in Dollimore 91)

Apocalyptic expectation characterized the religious climate in England from the Reformation until the Civil War. William Perkins composed a dialogue in 1587 discussing the popular conviction that the end was at hand, listing the signs of imminent Apocalypse, but concluding that "to divine of things to come, belongeth to God alone" ("Dialogue" 476). A flood of pamphlets predicted the final event in 1588; both Donne and Milton referred to "these latter days" (*Iuvenilia* F4v; *Works* 5: 307; both qtd. in Ball 23, 89). In such a climate, the afterlife obviously gained an immediate relevance. Fervent discussion of the characteristics of glorified bodies, for instance, flourished at this time.[2] Deep-seated anxieties set loose by the Reformation were absorbed and contained by the theater. Tragedy, in Frank Kermode's estimate, managed to "absorb the terrors of Apocalypse" (*Ending* 27). Stephen Greenblatt, concerned like Raymond Williams with the historical moment of Shakespearean drama, sees the rise of dramatic tragedy as intimately related to attitudes and occurrences within orthodoxy:

> At the moment when the official religious and secular institutions were, for their own reasons, abjuring the rituals

---

2. For descriptions of glorified bodies, see Day, Brightman, and Bullinger. Gifford and Bolton caution readers not to be curious about glorified bodies, while offering explicit assurance that "at the resurrection all shall be perfect" (Gifford 405).

they themselves had once fostered, Shakespeare's theater moves to appropriate this function. ("Exorcists" 181)

Greenblatt writes specifically of exorcism here, but the argument has implications for the Anglican version of afterlife as well. Whereas purgatory and the doctrine of saints had familiarized and familialized the afterlife, the more impersonal and imprecise Protestant doctrines about heaven opened an emotional void that dramatic romance could partially fill. One way of understanding Shakespeare's reunion scenes is to recognize the traces of a recalcitrant hope for reunion with the dead. But while Greenblatt's rhetoric here implies an opposition between the Church and theater, with the latter territorially "appropriating" rituals that the former had "abjured," I see a more reciprocal, mutually reinforcing, relationship between the two cultural institutions, such as that Greenblatt proposes in his later work. In *Shakespearean Negotiations*, he rejects a reflection model of the relation between theater and society for one of "dynamic exchange" (11).

Louis Montrose, assessing the Shakespearean drama's ability to perform cultural work, identifies three functions: "to neutralize social discontent; to assuage personal anxieties; and to provoke critical reflection upon the nature of society and the self" (65). It is important to move beyond seeing how "the public theatre absorbs some vital functions of ritual within Shakespeare's society" (Montrose 64) to noticing the possibilities intrinsic to the particular cultural forms. Theater offers word, spectacle, and bodily image, whereas the Church for the most part offers text alone. Although Shakespeare's dramaturgy has definitely quasi-liturgical qualities, the difference in mode has clear determining effects on the content expressed by the two institutions. Hermione's restoration supplements—"fleshes out"—the Church's somewhat equivocal promise of restored community in heaven. But the audience is led to make further distinctions between the offerings of the Church and theater because belief functions in different ways within each.

6

Sixteen years' absence has virtually the effect of death, on stage as in life. When Hermione is restored to Leontes, *The*

Winter's Tale becomes an image of heaven as Leontes at least might wish it. Frye, who understands romance generically as involving a "search for some kind of imaginative golden age" (*Anatomy* 186), calls the ending of *The Winter's Tale* "not so much an object of belief so much as an imaginative model of desire" (*Perspective* 117). It is not "her sainted spirit" (5.1.57) nor her "ghost" (5.1.63), but Hermione herself, "she [Leontes] kill'd" (5.1.15), who now "embraces him" (5.3.111). The play closes with a family reunion, the company exiting to learn from one another what has been "perform'd in this wide gap of time, since first / [They] were dissever'd" (5.3.154–55). The scene heals severed marriage and broken family ties, and Hermione's soul is reinstated in the statue that Leontes' coldness, in effect, made of her.

The severance of time itself, however, will not be healed. Most notably, Hermione has grown wrinkled, as Leontes mentions. The audience, even while it is caught in the joyous tide of re-union, is inevitably struck by how much has been lost in those sixteen years.

The image of reunion with the dead arrives in the theater still illuminated by religious awe. But dramatizing reunion with a woman supposedly dead for sixteen years has the insidiously ironic effect of making her return seem an equivocal gift. Leontes still seems unworthy; Hermione remains silent; some question if the reunion is a blessing at all. The fulfilled ideal offered to Leontes is very different from typically pallid Renaissance descriptions that exclude from heaven almost everything most people consider worth having on earth. Yet the reunion also shows the danger of an earthly image of heaven, for tainted as it is by time and human culpability, it will not bear transference beyond the closing words of the play. The image offers a kind of imaginative fulfillment but offers nothing to believe in but the power of theater. An audience may rejoice for the reunion in *The Winter's Tale* without being inclined to accept the image of reunion as something to hope for or to believe in. Mainly, the audience is aware of having constructed something upon which to rejoice.

The effect of the statue scene then, is like that Greenblatt attributes to *King Lear:* "to make us love the theater" ("Exorcists" 183). On stage, Shakespeare realized, we can see our desires fulfilled, safely cordoned from reality. Only in the theater can "playing dead" equal "being dead"; only here can we see the dead resurrected. The fantasy, or hope, of reunion with the dead can enjoy a permanent home in Shakespeare's theater, where a character's body always coexists with his or her soul, since both live only on the stage.

4
Pericles *and the Cosmic Overview*

Whereby I see that Time's the king of men,
He's both their parent and he is their grave,
And gives them what he will, not what they crave.
—Pericles

At the conclusions of Shakespeare's major tragedies, time is typically emptied of promise and meaning: "We that are young / Shall never see so much, nor live so long" (*Lr.* 5.3.326–27). Even if the conclusion means, as in *Macbeth*, that finally "the time is free" (*Mac.* 5.9.21), such freedom has a hollow, empty quality, for it is achieved at the cost of ethical certainty and with human bloodshed. One central concern in the romances is the discovery of a fruitful relationship with time or at least of a reconciliation to its inevitable passage. The typically episodic plot and paratactic structure of narrative romance mimic the experience of living in linear time, in which events follow one another according to no apparent logic and without yielding to human control. In Shakespeare's dramatic romances, however, this linear model meets and partially yields to a cosmic perspective on time. "Was he trying to write tragedy from God's viewpoint instead of from man's?" asks Herbert McArthur (45; qtd. in Mowat 5). The presence of Time itself as a character in *The Winter's Tale*, the sixteen-year gaps in both *Pericles* and *The Winter's Tale*, and Prospero's rigorous control of the minutes in *The Tempest* are all maneuvers to subdue time—not only dramatic time but also the real experience it imitates. The resurrections in the plays likewise subvert mortality, generally the hardest fact of temporal existence to accept. As Peterson suggests, these theatrical stratagems for coping with time all exhibit an artificial quality (62). The romances treat time itself as an artifact, an element in the dramatist's hands.

Pericles is the first of the romances, the most medieval, and by almost all accounts, the least satisfactory of the four plays. *Pericles*

61

is especially interesting, however, for the way it accomplishes a transference from tragic to romantic genres. The direct conflicts and finalities of tragedy are softened in *Pericles* under the lengthened perspective of dramatic romance, its essentially eschatological viewpoint. The play marks the intersection of tragedy's timebound world with the timeless vision of romance. This intersection is responsible for the aspects of *Pericles* considered most troubling—the peculiar structure and the jolting intrusions of the moralistic Gower.

Modern readers, accustomed to causal action in drama, have been frustrated by the sparse or unlikely connections between events in *Pericles*. But one of the play's central oddities has been insufficiently noticed: it consists of seven stretches of action demarcated by choric interruptions. Hoeniger considers it "highly doubtful whether *Pericles* was planned . . . as a five-act drama." He conjectures that instead it was "intended either as a play in two parts," noting that it was staged thus at Whitehall in 1619 with a refreshment break in the middle, or as "seven tableaux or acts, each separated by a chorus" (Introduction lii, lxvi).[1] Because modern editors present the text in five acts, its significant structure is obscured.

Moreover, the audience's perception of the course of events befalling Pericles and his family—the events generally assumed to be the play's main content—is repeatedly interrupted by the Chorus, Gower. Recently, the effect of Gower's presence in the play has received attention. Richard Hillman, for instance, reviews "the issue of [Gower's] mediation: does the Chorus create alienation or engagement, and exactly how?" ("Shakespeare's Gower" 427). My thesis is that Gower's intrusions compel the audience to dissociate itself from Pericles' adventures, to view the events as might God or an author or Gower himself. The structure of the play, considered from this vantage point, manifests notions of temporality rooted in a medieval metaphysic. The stages of Pericles' life mirror the structure of a symbolic history of the human race. An audience attuned to a figural view of reality, especially an audience retaining memories of the structure of the mystery cycles, might glimpse the skeletal

---

1. I have dealt with the structural issues in more detail in "The Seven Ages of *Pericles*," *Journal of the Rocky Mountain Medieval and Renaissance Society* 8 (1987): 147–62.

pattern of the medieval notion of the Seven Ages of History that lies beneath the action of *Pericles.*

1

To consider eschatology is perforce to consider structure. Only when events are viewed in their totality can "last things" be recognized as last, and the act of viewing events in their totality leads to imposition of structure onto the sequence. Expectations can powerfully alter perception, causing a sequence of events to appear differently once a specific conclusion is posited. A string of occurrences may seem random until the "sense of an ending" causes the sequence to resolve itself into the semblance of a pattern. Once established in the viewer's mind, such a pattern may be denied or detained or fulfilled, but it will almost invariably prevail as "structure." *Waiting for Godot* provides a modern example of a playwright's exploiting the way expectations produce structure. We perceive dramatic structure in part because we expect it, accepting generally neat editorial divisions of Shakespeare's plays into five acts with appropriate climaxes and denouements. In the Middle Ages, expectation of an orderly climax to history produced an analogous structure: history was composed of seven ages, delineated by a precise and careful deity.

Medieval conceptions of historical patterning derived largely from St. Augustine, whose thought "embodied the idea of the progressive self-revelation of God within history" (Reeves 40). God's involvement sanctified earthly time, but also invalidated any purely human historical progress. Time was redeemed by purpose, although the purpose itself was by most accounts imperceptible to humankind.

Augustine basically elaborates the analogies between God's authorship of history and his own authorship of a text when he concludes *The City of God* as well as the *Confessions* with meditative references to "the kingdom which has no end." He describes the eternal kingdom as temporal successor to earthly history. Yet in order to outline the course of cosmic time, which consists of six ages of human history, the sixth "now in progress," Augustine must assume for himself an eternal vantage point. Through an authorial act of self-transcendence, he removes himself from his time-bound existence in the sixth age and surveys history as he supposes God might. Thus he can predict that the seventh age will be the great sabbath, whose "end will not be an evening, but the Lord's Day, an eighth eternal day" (*City* 22.30). The pattern of the Seven Ages derives from the week of creation in Genesis; it is also implicit in other biblical verses (Gen. 5.1, 6.9; Matt. 1.1–17).

Augustine was intensely aware of the way words mark the passage of time (*Confessions* 11.28). Accordingly, he finds in his text's conclusion an image of mutability and mortality: the end of a book prefigures the end of all time. With his imaginative leap from within human history to an eternal viewpoint outside time, he accomplishes the authorial task of establishing his work as artifact. Analogously to the way a text moves from sequential production into artistic permanence, the process of time (history) becomes an artifact (the Seven Ages) under God's shaping hands.

For Augustine and for those who inherited his metaphysical assumptions, adopting God's eschatological viewpoint presupposed the dual metaphysical order of Boethius, with its parallel divine and mundane planes of reality. Shakespeare goes "beyond tragedy" (Uphaus 1, 3) by partially returning to this figural medieval world view, according to which dramatic occurrences in human life result from "a change of fortune breaking in upon man from without and from above" (Auerbach 318). Ricardo Quinones points the general distinction between medieval and Renaissance attitudes toward time:

> For the Middle Ages time could be abundant because behind the chances and changes of events man could sense a higher directing order. His life still had religious associations with the universe, his beginnings and his end were in the hands of a providential and concerned divinity. . . . But for the new men of the Renaissance time was not plentiful but rare and precious. Since it was constantly slipping away, man must utilize available means of controlling it and, in some measure, ward off the termination it promoted. . . . The more of his own experience the individual managed to control, the more he mastered by his own skill, the less inclined he would be to let things be, to rely with patient trust in a providential Creator. (7–8)

The heroes of Renaissance tragedy assume, or are charged with, major responsibility for their own destinies. For Shakespeare, going beyond tragedy means reassigning control of destiny to forces "above" or "beyond" the human plane. But the romances do not deliver human fate wholesale into the hands of fortune, nor are they simply Christian allegory. Instead they suggest a complex interplay of temporal and eternal purposes in human life.

The Boethian metaphysic requires dual consideration of human life from temporal and eternal perspectives. The story of Pericles' life, for instance, seems tragic (why must he wait so long for redemption from sorrow?) or simply meaningless, when viewed from a temporal perspective; it resembles a string of chance misfortunes yielding inexplicably to good luck at the last. "Life itself, the play seems to imply, is mainly episodic" (Peterson 80). From a projected eternal perspective, however, these adventures mirror the Seven Ages into which human history was divided by virtually every Christian historian and chronicler prior to Shakespeare's day. From this perspective, Pericles becomes exemplary; his story illustrates that hidden patterns may shape even the most apparently random order of events. *Pericles* serves as a kind of metaphysical exercise, inviting the audience to assess the significance of the hero's life, his place in the universe. The play is uniquely designed to incorporate the symbolic history of the human race into the history of one man.

2

Gower is charged with mediating temporal and eternal perspectives on the action in *Pericles*. As "Shakespeare's means of controlling audience perspective" (Peterson 72), Gower tempers immediate response to the action with his moral commentary, which urges distance. Yet he is a partially unstable and in many ways unsatisfactory mediator. The patent inadequacy and impracticality of many of his interpretive suggestions prompt the audience also to consider other perspectives for interpreting the actions on stage. Shakespeare's "abstraction of history" here resembles the strategy Wittreich perceives in *King Lear:* he "ambiguates history by complicating its patterns and multiplying perspectives on it" (35).

The Chorus betrays a remarkably cavalier attitude toward time throughout *Pericles:*

> Be attent,
> And time that is so briefly spent
> With your fine fancies quaintly eche.
> (3.Cho.11–13)

> Thus time we waste, and long leagues make short.
> (4.4.1)

> Now our sands are almost run,
> More a little, and then dumb.
> (5.2.1–2)

With these comments Gower indicates how dramatic time lies at his disposal as he narrates the tale. But more importantly, he reveals himself free from temporal constraints. According to the play's fiction, he is a visitor from the dead, deliberately resurrected to present this story:

> To sing a song that old was sung,
> From ashes ancient Gower is come,
> Assuming man's infirmities,
> To glad your ear and please your eyes.
> (1.Cho.1–4)

The Chorus has "assum[ed] man's infirmities"—put on a mortal body—in order to relate his didactic tale more convincingly. Earthly time is arbitrary for the visitor from the eternal realm:

> If you, born in these latter times,
> When wit's more ripe, accept my rhymes,
> And that to hear an old man sing
> May to your wishes pleasure bring,
> I life would wish, and that I might
> Waste it for you like taper-light.
> (1.Cho.11–16)

Gower disdains earthly time—wastes it "like taper-light"—because he has achieved the perspective of providential time.

The notion of double time adumbrates the structure of the Boethian cosmology, which accomplishes a reconciliation of fortune and providence. According to Boethius, fortune, or the course of earthly affairs, is ordered by an omniscient God, who "sees what is fitting for each individual, and arranges what he knows is fitting" (365). From the earthly viewpont, the providential order seems to be the random turning of fortune's wheel.

If people could achieve the divine perspective, however, they "would judge that there was no evil anywhere" (371) in the work of fortune. Boethius asserts that human understanding is hampered only by temporal limitation:

> For whatever lives in time proceeds in the present from the past into the future, and there is nothing established in time which can embrace the whole space of its life equally. . . . [But God] is permanent in the simplicity of his present, and embracing all the infinite spaces of the future and the past, [God] considers them in his simple act of knowledge as though they were now going on. (423, 427)

The Boethian God exists in a virtually dialectical relation to time. While himself outside the temporal flux, he joins it in an "embrace," which constitutes the revelation of divine will in history.

Gower could serve a Jacobean audience appropriately as instructor on Boethian concepts of providence. The historical John Gower's *Confessio Amantis* was modeled on Boethius' *The Consolation of Philosophy*. In the *Confessio*, John Gower emphasizes the directive role of Fortune in his story of Apollonius (the source for *Pericles*):

> Fortune hath evere be muable
> And mai no while stonde stable:
> For now it hiheth, now it loweth,
> Now stant upriht, now overthroweth,
> Now full of blisse and now of bale,
> As in the tellinge of mi tale.
> (412; 8.585–90)

The *Confessio* also makes reference to the Seven Ages. For instance, the prologue to book 8, which contains the Apollonius tale, traces the history of incest through the first three ages, those of Adam, Noah, and Abraham.

These more strictly medieval attitudes are modified in Shakespeare's picture of Gower. The Chorus emphasizes in *Pericles* the provisional nature of fortune. He comments on the limited understanding of the hero:

> Let Pericles believe his daughter's dead,
> And bear his courses to be ordered
> By Lady Fortune. . . .
> (4.4.46–48)

67

Pericles is allowed temporarily to believe a random or even malevolent fortune to be operant in his life, although ultimately this view is corrected. In his epilogue to the play, Gower explicitly notes the relationship between fortune and heaven, observing that Pericles and his family, "although assail'd with fortune fierce and keen," were "led on by heaven, and crown'd with joy at last" (Epi. 4, 6). The Chorus of Shakespeare's play affirms a central controlling force in the play, beside which "fortune," the apparent randomness of events, is secondary.

The author of a text, like the Boethian God, foresees the promised end of his work and arranges events in accordance with that foreordained future. By resurrecting Gower and allowing him to present his tale to the audience, Shakespeare provides a theatrical image of the author as creator. Even though Gower acknowledges the antiquity of his tale (1.Cho.5–8) and denies actual originality ("I tell you what mine authors say" [1.Cho.20]), he is scarcely the mere spectator he sometimes pretends to be. Not only does he interpret the tale, but he is privy to information denied the theatrical audience; his choruses frequently introduce new facts. Gower suggests that he views Pericles' adventures in their totality, but presents only selected episodes of the life history on stage. At 4.Cho.6, for instance, "our fast-growing scene must find" a mature Marina at Tharsus, where she was left as an infant only one scene previously. Similarly at 4.4.9–10, Gower reports that "Pericles / Is now again thwarting the wayward seas," suggesting that the hero has taken to sea offstage, that Gower merely discovers him. At 5.Cho.12–13, the Chorus directs "our thoughts again" to Pericles, "where we left him, on the sea." The hero has been absent from the audience's sight but not, evidently, from Gower's. The Chorus reports Pericles "arriv'd / Here where his daughter dwells" (5.Cho.14–15). Gower ostensibly presents on stage only a portion of the complete life of Pericles, of which he alone has full knowledge, much as God alone, according to Boethianism, can survey human actions in their totality. Gower, then, is an intermediary not just between audience and action, but between temporal and eternal perspectives:

> I do beseech you
> To learn of me, who stand i' th' gaps to teach you
> The stages of our story.
>
> (4.4.7–9)

Gower's authorial omniscience and his suggestion of a foreordained action assert a central commissioning intelligence ordering the play's paradigmatic structure. A play that bears the marks of two authorial hands might well have taken recourse to some such paradigm, an overarching pattern that allows for diffuseness of individual parts by confirming their meaning through relationship to the general framework.[2]

3

Everything about Gower would have seemed old-fashioned to a Jacobean audience—the antiquated role of Chorus, his tetrameter couplets and archaic diction, possibly his appearance (Hoeniger, "Gower and Shakespeare" 463–64). So his very presence suggests a medieval response, reinforcing the medieval world view he preaches. The archaeologically produced notion of double time is conveyed through the discrepancy between Pericles' attitude toward his adventures while they are taking place (the attitude largely shared by the audience) and Gower's view of those adventures from his timeless perspective as dead soul and as author. As Peterson observes, "When the play is over and we have reflected upon [it], we should be able to perceive that the play itself is a complex emblem" (72).[3] The play's structure mimics the discrepancy in human experience between the apparently meaningless sequences of events that compose a lifetime, and the structure of meaning informing that life which would appear from a cosmic perspective. According to Christian historians, such a pattern of meaning is present continuously to God and would be available to everyone at Doomsday when the order of human life was finally and completely manifested.

God's purposes may be mysterious, but the pattern of the

2. The major theories regarding the authorship question are found in articles by Kenneth Muir and Philip Edwards. Hoeniger reviews the case in his Arden introduction. With regard to a structural plan, Phyllis Gorfain observes how "a structural approach especially suits this work, particularly since it may be applied independently of textual issues" (11).

3. The emblem Peterson detects is one of "love's restorative power in a fallen world" (72). He finds the play's action to be divided into four sections, each containing a trial of the hero's faith.

Seven Ages posits a discernible divine order shaping history. The major variation on Augustine's world week was that introduced by Joachim of Fiore in the twelfth century. Joachim shared Augustine's basic framework but believed that the "pattern of history was as yet incomplete"; he differed from Augustine in placing the Seventh Age, the great sabbath, within history (Reeves 49–50). Joachim's scheme enhanced the importance of earthly history. This secular valuation was increasingly evident, and eventually the medieval expectation of imminent Apocalypse, which had been fanned to open fire by the Reformation, was converted into "belief in a future golden age" on earth (Capp 101).

But throughout the Middle Ages and the Renaissance, the preeminence of the pattern of the Seven Ages was indisputable. The popular *Golden Legend* outlines the ages like this:

> The first is from Adam to Noah; the second from Noah to Abraham; the third from Abraham to Moses; the fourth from Moses unto David; the fifth from David to Jesu Christ. The sixth from Jesu Christ unto the end of the world. The seventh of the dying on earth. And the eighth of the general resurrection to heaven. (1: 37)

The different versions which developed were similar enough that each age evolved its hero in the popular mind, a major figure who became the symbol for his entire era. And in each scheme a new age typically begins with a fresh covenant between God and his people, an event that marks a significant manifestation of divine will in the course of human affairs, and so alters the previous course of history.

Pericles explores time's doubleness, the interplay of eternity and temporality, by dramatizing one exemplary figure's history. Felperin thus cites the miracle plays, or saints' lives, as its dramatic precedents (*Romance* 150–51). Also, Hoeniger traces some remarkable parallels between *Pericles* and *Mary Magdalene* (Introduction lxxxviii–xci). Despite its scenic and thematic ties with the miracle plays, however, the structure of *Pericles* recalls another type of medieval drama, the mystery cycles. Ambitious in scope, the cycles enacted the whole of human history, from Creation to Doomsday. In order to give form to this mass of material, history was viewed from a cosmic, eschatological perspective. From this vantage point, two patterns connecting earthly events emerged: biblical typology and the Seven Ages of History (Kolve 57–100). Typology finds individual events meaningful not only in themselves, but as prefigurations of later events or figurations of earlier ones. Abraham's near-sacrifice of Isaac is important because it demonstrates patriarchal faith, but even more because it prefigures God's sacrifice of Christ. Such figural relationships carry almost causal weight, for typology assumes a foreordained order in history. But perceiving these relationships necessitates a long view of history, since figures are ultimately connected in the timeless eye and mind of God.

The Corpus Christi cycles show history to be meaningful only in light of its created beginning and its apocalyptic ending. Within this linear temporal structure, however, history is shown to be cyclical. Typology emphasizes the repetition of certain key motifs at different points in the pattern. Cycles are also marked by the periodic interventions of divine will. The mystery plays are unconcerned with the profane duration of years between epiphanies; they dramatize only those moments when God alters the course of human events.

Typology and the theory of the Seven Ages shape history through reference to a timeless realm. The mystery cycle plays show human time to be an artifact, God's dramatic masterpiece. Humanity's goal, encouraged by the plays, was to disdain the present and strive for a cosmic perspective whereby God's hand could be traced in history. Because the events enacted in the mystery cycles derive significance through eternal reference, rather than through direct relation with each other, "the progression from episode to episode" lacks "consecutive impulse" for "it is not built on a theory of direct causation" (Kolve 119). The mystery cycles provide one model for representing people as both historical creatures living in linear time and transcendent beings who identify themselves by reference to an eternal realm. The two realms of existence intersect at those moments when the history of Israel is altered by God's intervention, as in the parting of the Red Sea or the birth of Christ, or when humanity defines itself in opposition or obedience to God's command, as when Eve bites the apple or Mary accepts Gabriel's message. The overall sequence becomes a meaningful pattern only through reference to the eternal realm. A concrete pattern is manifested in history; history expresses God's dialogue through time with the human race. But lack of compelling plot connections between dramatized events makes the structure of the cycles episodic, and presentation of individual plays on pageant wagons would have emphasized such separateness.

Pericles is criticized for a similar lack of organic development and causal connection between its episodes. Human actions and their consequences form the basis for most modern conceptions of drama. In Pericles, by contrast, action is initiated from without, by chance, fortune, or providence. It is possible to discover patterns in Pericles' life, such as Leech's life-cycle (22), or the general felix culpa design various critics have seen (Felperin, Romance 167; Hunter 140–41; Knight 73–74; Traversi 40). As corollaries of the scheme of Seven Ages, these patterns exhibit interesting parallels with Erik Erikson's stages of human development (247–74); the recurrence of the scheme in modern psychology suggests its typal force. In applying such patterns to drama, the problem that must be addressed is their virtual invisibility while the action is taking place. In order to glimpse any pattern, a final perspective, such as that assumed toward earthly history by the Corpus Christi cycles, by Augustine, and by Christian historians, is necessary. A theory of the structure of Pericles is needed that both delivers a meaningful pattern and explains its obfuscation.

While Pericles traces the lifetime of one man, it also seems to outline the history of the human race. The correspondences between the individual and the cosmos that were intrinsic to Renaissance ontology make this structural appropriation natural. A connection between the ages of history and those of humankind was by no means original. Augustine himself had drawn a specific analogy between the growth from infancy of an individual and the developmental history of God's people (City 16.43). The Venerable Bede followed Augustine in relating the historical ages to man's "infancy," "childhood," "adolescence," "youth," "senility," and "decrepit old age," leading the faithful to "the seventh age of one endless Sabbath" and expectation of the "eighth age of a happy resurrection" (220–21). In the visual arts, the two sequences were frequently brought together, as in a twelfth-century stained glass at Canterbury Cathedral that shows the miracle at Cana bordered on one side by the six ages of human life and on the other side by the six ages of the world (Kolve 89–90).

Shakespeare expresses the microcosmic form of the Seven

Ages in Jaques' famous soliloquy in *As You Like It*, where the ages of an individual's life are compared to seven acts of a play.[4] No matter what play (if any) Shakespeare had in mind, John Bale's publication in 1538 of "A Tragedy or Interlude manifesting the chief promises of God unto man by all ages in the old law" (reissued 1577) provides interesting evidence that such plays did exist. Since Bale was a fiery Reformation commentator, his prominent use of the scheme establishes its Protestant usage.

Pericles does not follow the seven ages of an individual's lifetime (infant, child, adolescent, etc.). Instead it makes innovative use of a familiar set of traditions by incorporating the symbolic history of the human race into the history of one man. The play explores existence in time by epitomizing cosmic history in a single lifetime. The audience experiences the interplay between Gower's extratemporal vision and the more limited earthly vision of the hero himself. Because the play insists on the interplay between microcosmic and macrocosmic levels, the hero's personal experience merges with, or recapitulates, biblical history. Considering an extended life history perhaps prompted the analogy with a pattern shaping all of human history.

The Seven Ages exist as a skeleton beneath the play's action, and recognition of the scheme should be considered a necessary prolegomenon to *Pericles*. The existence of this shaping pattern does not mean that individual scenes are fundamentally different in construction than they would be in a play with a more dynamic plot. Rather, the scheme's influence is felt in the distinctive pattern of theme and image found in the seven sequences. As in the cycle plays, episodes are meaningful for the way they fit into the overall framework. Recognition of the divisions themselves, which demands adoption of the Boethian perspective, is more important than recognizing the peculiar motif of any individual age, even though the two endeavors are clearly interdependent. The pattern of Seven Ages exerts a quiet but distinctive force on the structure of *Pericles*, similar to that Kolve perceives in the mystery cycles, none of which "openly develops the theme,"

---

4. See Michael J. B. Allen on the traditions of astronomical and astrological correspondences with the Seven Ages of Man. Allen is concerned, as I am, with various associations Shakespeare's audience might have had with the familiar paradigm, rather than with articulation of any particular source.

although "it has undoubtedly caused the Corpus Christi drama to find a distinctive protocycle core" (99).

The relevant parallels in *Pericles* tend to occur near the beginning of each episode, thereby introducing the motif of a particular age. Correspondences with some ages are closer than with others. The first section of *Pericles* carries unmistakable resonances of the myth of the Fall, but the fifth section corresponds only loosely with the Age of David. (However, the fifth age was a trouble spot in schemes of the Seven Ages. David was usually considered as symbolic of all the prophets. In one alternative version, the captivity of the Israelites in Babylon is the significant event of the fifth age, but their captivity produced no "hero" in the popular mind.) To an audience familiar with the Seven Ages, the pattern would be established as soon as the first episode with its echoes of the Fall was followed by an action recalling the story of Noah. Why, then, have critics failed to notice the pattern before? For two reasons, I think: first, an unreliable text has discouraged sustained critical attention; and second, modern assumptions of a five-act structure have obscured the play's pattern of seven episodes.

4

The significant action of the first age is of course the Fall. Pericles' first adventure in Antioch involves the discovery of knowledge (deciphering the riddle) and the concomitant discovery of sin (recognizing Antiochus' incestuous relationship with his daughter). According to the law of the kingdom, the price for Pericles' misdeed—his discovery—is death. The Antioch episode is rich in imagery suggesting the myth of the Fall. Felperin notes an allusion to "the myth of Eden and the fall into knowledge ("Miracle Play" 366); Hillman mentions Pericles' "naive use of the symbolism of the Fall" ("Romance" 150). Pericles speaks of "gods"

> that have inflam'd desire in my breast
> To taste the fruit of yon celestial tree
> (Or die in th' adventure).
> (1.1.20–23)

Antiochus refers to his daughter as "this fair Hesperides, / With golden fruit, but dangerous to be touch'd" (1.1.27–28). Later, Pericles calls both father and daughter "serpents" (1.1.132). Al-

though Pericles does not himself partake of sin, the memory of
what he has discovered seems to haunt him; after fleeing Antioch
he is unable to shake "the sad companion, dull-ey'd melancholy"
(1.2.3). His subsequent flight from the threat of Antiochus' vengeance echoes the wanderings through the world of the fallen
Adam. And while Pericles is not actually condemned to labor
with sweat on his brow, he undergoes a sort of penance, "punish-
[ing] that before that [Antiochus] would punish" (1.2.33). Or as
Helicanus explains to the Tyrian lords, Pericles,

> doubting lest he had err'd or sinn'd,
> To show his sorrow, he'd correct himself;
> So puts himself unto the shipman's toil,
> With whom each minute threatens life or death.
> (1.3.21–24)

The hero's shipwreck off the coast of Pentapolis, with the stage
direction, "*Enter Pericles, wet*" (2.1.1sd), opens the play's second
age, corresponding to the Age of Noah. Pericles, having been
"wash'd . . . from shore to shore" (2.1.6), has learned the lesson
of mortality and he is, like Noah, obedient:

> Wind, rain, and thunder, remember earthly man
> Is but a substance that must yield to you;
> And I (as fits my nature) do obey you.
> (2.1.2–4)

The presence of the fishermen underlines the special importance
of the sea in this age. Fishermen were frequently connected
in biblical typology with Christ ("the fisher of men"), so their
presence here suggests the motif of redemption so central to the
second age, the age of the near-destruction of the human race.
The earthy good humor of these fishermen is perhaps reminiscent of the stock comedy provided by Noah's wife in the mystery
cycles. Like Noah after the flood, Pericles receives a promise of
better fortune after enduring loss and destruction. His fortune
turns when the rusty armor drawn up by the fishermen enables
him to compete for Thaisa's hand. The armor itself seems symbolic of faith; Pericles' description of it echoes the scriptural
" 'armor of the Lord' " (Hoeniger, *Pericles* 48–49n). Pericles
quotes his father's claim, "It hath been a shield / 'Twixt me and
death" (2.1.126–27).

The dumb show at the beginning of act 3 shows the court

of Simonides receiving news that its "heir-apparent is a king!" (3.Cho.37). With Antiochus dead, Pericles may set out to reclaim his kingdom, which becomes a kind of promised land for the destitute wanderer. This is the third age, that of Abraham. Pericles boards ship with a pregnant wife; her role is Sarah's, and in her the promise of generation is visually portrayed. Like Abraham, Pericles must be prepared to sacrifice a member of his family. He loses his wife instead of his child, but his words could be Abraham's on the Mount of Vision when Pericles demands of the gods, "Why do you make us love your goodly gifts / And snatch them straight away?" (3.1.23–24). Pericles exhibits a patriarchial faith when, bereft of his wife, he says:

> We cannot but obey
> The powers above us. Could I rage and roar
> As doth the sea she lies in, yet the end
> Must be as 'tis.
>
> (3.3.9–12)

The destruction of Antiochus and his daughter—"A fire from heaven came and shrivell'd up / Those bodies, even to loathing" (2.4.9–10)—suggests the burning of Sodom and Gomorrah. The brimstone that rained on the two towns (Gen. 19.24) was equated with sulfur in Shakespeare's time (*OED*). This king and his daughter "so stunk" (2.4.10) that their subjects refused to go near to bury them. Helicanus calls it "but justice" that "sin had his reward" (2.4.13, 15), and the sin is appropriately sexual. The report of Antiochus' death appears in the second section of *Pericles,* not the third, which corresponds to Abraham's age. Yet the report is distinctly background information, which might be provided almost anywhere (and given the tangled state of the existing text, a misplaced scene would not be surprising). Most relevant is the association between the place from which Pericles flees and the fate of Sodom and Gomorrah.

Attention shifts at the start of act 4 from Pericles to the mature Marina, illustrating well the lack of causal connections. Nothing in the previous action (other than the repetition of misfortune) leads one to expect a plot against Marina's life; and only a thematic concern with time dictates a dramatic jump over sixteen years. It is useful to recall Kolve's analysis of the structural basis of the cycles:

The events chosen for dramatization are those in which God intervenes in human history; significant time, it follows, becomes simply the point of intersection between these actions, the will of God expressed in time from outside time, by which a connection deeper than temporal causality is stated. (119)

In *Pericles*, events are ostensibly chosen for dramatization by Gower, the Chorus-presenter who is also the author, the creator, and hence the God of this secular drama. His choices manifest several basic medieval divisions of history, including that of the Three Laws—Natural Law, which governed the first three ages; Written Law, instituted by Moses and governing the fourth and fifth ages; and the Law Fulfilled, the law of charity ordained by Christ and governing the sixth and seventh ages.

The shift in focus to Marina with the fourth episode of *Pericles* corresponds to the institution of written law in the fourth age, the Age of Moses. Marina herself represents a new code, a different way of dealing with the world. The Age of Moses was represented in the cycle plays by both the presentation of the Decalogue and the dramatization of exile; the latter is particularly relevant to Marina, whose existence in Tharsus and Mytilene amounts to an exodus. (Her first speech in the play concludes, "This world to me is as a lasting storm, / Whirring me from my friends" [4.1.19–20].) Dionyza's plot to kill Marina, who is perceived as a threat to the Tharsian princess, recalls the Pharoah's slaughter of Hebrew children whom he perceived as a threat. Captive in the brothel in Mytilene (where she is described as "a sojourner" [4.2.136]), Marina is servant to corrupt people, and can rely only on her own faith.

Marina's period of preaching in Mytilene corresponds to the Age of the Prophets. While not exactly a prophet herself, she establishes a reputation for surprising conversions that damages the brothel's business, and she is described in semiprophetic terms, as the following dialogue indicates:

> 1. *Gent.* Did you ever hear the like?
> 2. *Gent.* No, nor never shall do in such a place as this, she being once gone.
> 1. *Gent.* But to have divinity preach'd there! did you ever dream of such a thing?

2. *Gent.* No, no. Come, I am for no more bawdy-houses.
Shall's go hear the vestals sing?
1. *Gent.* I'll do anything now that is virtuous. . . .

(4.5.1–8)

Marina's powers of speech are emphasized throughout this episode, not only by the Bawd, who says "she would make a puritan of the devil" (4.6.9), but also by the Governor Lysimachus:

I did not think
Thou couldst have spoke so well, ne'er dreamt thou couldst.
Had I brought hither a corrupted mind,
Thy speech had alter'd it.

(4.6.102–5)

Like Daniel in the lions' den, Marina in the brothel suffers a peculiar persecution, but remains steadfast.

The coming of Christ initiates the sixth age, which would, according to most chroniclers, extend over the entire Christian era up to the end of earthly history. The Incarnation marks another important division in history—that between the first dispensation, the time of justice, and the second, the time of mercy. Clearly the course of Pericles' life is altered with the sixth episode; for the first time, grace is apparent in his fortunes. The memorable image of the sixth section of *Pericles* is the vision of Diana, a manifestation of divinity in the world of the play and "the single symbolic image that expresses the whole play," in the words of John Arthos (265). Having heard "the music of the spheres" (5.1.229), Pericles is suddenly cast into "thick slumber" (5.1.234), and Diana reveals herself to him (and to the audience, in most productions). She directs him to her temple at Ephesus to make sacrifice and recite his story to the people there; clearly she directs him toward reunion with his lost wife. For the first time, the audience can perceive causal order in the events of the play; Pericles' history is being fulfilled, as human history was reaching fulfillment through Christ, according to religious historians. Diana wrests from the moribund Pericles a new promise of obedience; one could say they establish a new covenant. Marking a change in fortune, a coming of grace, for Pericles, the goddess' appearance functions analogously to Christ's alteration of the course of human history according to Christian doctrine. The vision, like Jupiter's descent in *Cymbeline*, is not exactly an allegory of the Incarnation, though it functions analogously. The vision gives an image of the descent of divine power into the world of the play, and hence breaks the boundaries between ordinary experience and the miraculous, between the profane and the sacred. Knight calls it a "breaking of those boundaries" that separate heavenly harmony from earthly decay (67). The vision reveals a shaping order in the course of Pericles' life, but the play is attuned to human desires. Reunion with daughter and wife count for far more than does the revelation of divinity in itself.

Hence the end—both goal and conclusion—of earthly history, the seventh age, Augustine's "great sabbath," is represented by the reunion of Pericles, Marina, and Thaisa in the temple of Diana. The scene is set apart from the rest of the play by its hushed tone of mystery. This reunion is more than Pericles could ever have hoped for, and the action is of a different magnitude from the previous adventures. So the seventh age, marking the beginning of eternity, stands against the preceding six ages of earthly time. Although Pericles and Thaisa have not actually died and risen blessed, the motif of death and resurrection pervades the scene at Ephesus:

> Did you not name a tempest,
> A birth, and death?
> (5.3.33–34)

> The voice of dead Thaisa!
> (5.3.34)

> O, come, be buried
> A second time within these arms.
> (5.3.43–44)

The audience's understanding of this reunion must include the memories of Thaisa entombed and cast overboard and of Pericles comatose until touched by Marina. Pericles and Thaisa have undergone years of suffering, for no crime but that of being mortal; they now are reborn to a redeemed experience of life that gives as well as takes away. The magnitude of Pericles' and Thaisa's sufferings makes them seem to represent something larger than themselves. The curious sequence of events in their story becomes a significant structure when they are viewed as figures who enact the destiny of the whole human race.

The seven episodes of *Pericles* in a sense recapitulate one another, for each follows a basic pattern in which Pericles or Marina faces some trial and either endures or receives a reprieve. The Seven Ages of History also repeat a basic action: significant to each age is the reestablishment of a covenant between God and humanity. This pattern is clearly seen in Bale's *God's Promises*, where the seven acts correspond to the Seven Ages, each beginning with a lament by God the Father over the sinful state of humankind and each culminating with a new covenant. A covenant, a promise, is something that may be fulfilled only in the future, and so the structure of the Seven Ages provides a forward-moving view of history. Medieval historians were compelled to place their own lives in the sixth age, thus merging history—the report of a known past—with a transcendent vision of the future provided by faith. *Pericles* demonstrates this eschatological approach to history, by incorporating the Boethian idea of double time into the play's structure. Shakespeare traces the hero's road to the eventual discovery that meaning and promise informed his life all along, and juxtaposes Gower's timeless perspective on that life. Gower knows, and Pericles learns, that through the consideration of ultimate ends one can achieve self-transcendence. Or as Peterson puts it, "By refusing to surrender to the view that events are random and therefore under the absolute domination of fortune, or that life is merely a matter of ripening and rotting, Pericles [and other characters in the romances] retain their freedom from the deterministic claims of nature" (32). Human existence thus ceases to be a linear sequence of unconnected events and becomes instead a significant conflict leading to redemption.

5

Thematically as well as structurally, ideas of time and eternity dominate *Pericles*. Since Gower alone has full knowledge of time's outcome, the other characters are necessarily concerned with the qualities required to deal with temporal existence. Temporal existence here, as in *King Lear*, means tragic existence, and patience is crucial in both plays. Lear, on the edge of madness, pleads, "You Heavens, give me that patience, patience I need!" (*Lr.* 2.4.271). Both Lychorida and Helicanus entreat Pericles to have patience, and evidently he holds that virtue in great esteem, for the highest compliment he can pay to Marina in the moment of their reunion is to evoke the emblem of "Patience gazing on kings' graves, and smiling / Extremity out of act" (*Per.* 5.1.138–39). Echoing *Twelfth Night*'s "Patience on a monument, / Smiling at grief" (*TN* 2.4.114–15), the line suggests an emblem such as Ripa's Patienza, who smiles and sits on a block that resembles a tomb. Philip Brockbank points out the image's particularly "disquieting" power here, since "Pericles looks almost literally like one rising from the grave" (115). Knight attributes to patience the power to transcend tragedy:

> The whole world of great tragedy ("kings' graves") is subdued to an over-watching figure, like Cordelia's love by the bedside of Lear's sleep. "Extremity," that is disaster in all its finality (with perhaps a further suggestion of endless time) is therefore negated, put out of action, by a serene assurance corresponding to St. Paul's certainty in "O death, where is thy sting?" Patience is here an all-enduring calm seeing *through* tragedy to the end; smiling through endless death to ever-living eternity. (15)

Knight implies something more by patience than mere stoic endurance. His definition suggests a future orientation, like St. Paul's "ye have nede of pacience, that after ye have done the wil of God, ye might receive the promes" (Heb. 10.36). Patience in this sense is an expression of hope, which renders the future— be it "ever-living eternity," "the promes," or reunion with a lost child—available now, in the present, as it were on loan from the future. By providing a means to endure present suffering, hope can be a life-giving doctrine. And hope must precede the kind of Christian patience Knight refers to, since hope's forward-looking orientation allows transcendence of the present moment and thus an escape from the relentless linearity of historical time.

Complementary to the emblem of patience in *Pericles* is one of hope. In the tournament scene, six knights present their various devices. Sources or analogues have been discovered in contemporary emblem books for each device but that of Pericles:

> His present is
> A withered branch, that's only green at top;
> The motto: "*In Hac spe vivo.*"
> (2.2.42–44)

81

It has been suggested that Pericles offers an actual withered branch rather than a painted device (Knight 47). The motto "in this hope I live" labels the power of faith at work in the scene: Pericles, "the mean knight," competes in rusty armor salvaged from a wreck, and wins.

The emblems of patience and hope stand in conjunction, indicating two poles of a faithful attitude toward life. In a world where meanings are mysterious, one requires patience to endure the battery of sufferings and hope that misfortunes will not prove finally senseless. The complementarity of patience and hope, peculiarly time-oriented virtues, correspond with Boethian double time: tied to the earthly vision of limits and chronicity, people are promised a glimpse of the saving force of time.

The timeless perspective in *Pericles* afforded by the Chorus Gower and the structural embodiment of a microcosmic human history together suggest that a dual vision is required to judge the play. From the earthly perspective of tragedy, the hero is a victim of fortune, a fool of time. This vision is entirely legitimate, since Pericles' despair and suffering may remain more accessible to the audience than the joy and wonder of the reunion scenes. But at the play's end Gower's timeless perspective becomes more generally available, and by viewing Pericles' life in its totality, order appears in a mad universe, pattern replaces parataxis, cycles of time replace crises.

The commonly voiced complaint that *Pericles* is uneven in dramatic intensity is justified. While several scenes in the play, especially the reunion of Pericles and Marina, contain a beauty and suggestive power approaching that of *King Lear*, the play exhibits no sustained immediacy, and the response to this has been disappointment. It is time to realize that the structure of *Pericles*, obscured by the editorial assumption of five dramatic acts, suggests a reason and purpose for the play's rebuffing of sympathy. The pattern of history's ages and the eternal perspective of Gower both work to pull the audience back from the action, away from sympathetic touch with the characters. Shakespeare, having explored in the great tragedies the disastrous attempts of individuals to order human life, recoiled from this sensibility in the last plays. The duality of time contemplated in *Pericles* and illustrated in its incorporation of the pattern of the Seven Ages signals an approach to the problem of human suffering that derived largely from a medieval perspective.

6

Although *Pericles* is dominated for the most part by spectacle and narrative, an evident plot surfaces near the end when the king finds his family. The emergence of guided destiny from the midst of apparent formlessness is even stronger here than in *Cymbeline*, where the convergence of parallel destinies also allows characters to find each other. The conclusions of both plays give a strong sense of providential guidance; the virtual equation of plot with providence in *Pericles* is particularly striking. The passage of time in the hero's life becomes not only opportune but provident near the end. After Pericles' reunion with Marina, the action makes provision for the future and in fact races toward it. The progress from the vision of Diana to the reunion at Ephesus is swift and unencumbered.

Despite the sense in the last scene of propulsion into the future (a movement and attitude ordinarily associated with the attempt to devour inimical time), time itself here becomes, as never before in Pericles' experience, filled with promise. His characteristic passivity yields to joyous anticipation of the future:

> Now do I long to hear how you were found,
> How possibly preserved, and who to thank,
> (Besides the gods) for this great miracle.
> (5.3.56–58)

> Will you deliver
> How this dead queen relives?
> (5.3.63–64)

> Pure Dian,
> I bless thee for thy vision, and will offer
> Night-oblations to thee.
> (5.3.68–70)

> there, my queen,
> We'll celebrate their nuptials, and ourselves
> Will in that kingdom spend our following days.
> (5.3.79–81)

Pericles' idiom is dominated by the future tense, in a fruitful contrast to the scene's basic retrospectivity (reunion, re-living). His spiritual rebirth has altered his experience of time itself, from perception of the corruption of devouring passage to the salvific ordering of destiny. Or put another way, he has entered the seventh age, where, according to Augustine, earthly time ceases to exist, where past, present, and future are simultaneously experienced. The seventh age, the postapocalyptic world, was considered humanity's future state but a state that paradoxically obliterates all temporal distinctions.

Destiny in *The Winter's Tale* is attributed to the oracle of Apollo, which functions as an ordering force of ambiguous significance in the play. Apollo allegedly controls the action in the play. Hermione believes "pow'rs divine / Behold our human actions" (3.2.28–29), while Leontes attributes Mamillius' death to Apollo's anger: "The heavens themselves / Do strike at my injustice" (3.2.146–47). Yet the god in *The Winter's Tale* scants the sort of visceral force that Jupiter, descending to Posthumus' prison cell, exerts in *Cymbeline*, or the certain thematic appropriateness that makes Diana a crucial presence in *Pericles*. The world of *The Winter's Tale* operates independently of the gods for the most part, although the oracle provides this secular world with a degree of clarity and imposed meaning. At the very least, the oracle functions prophetically, providing continuity of past, present, and future by indicating a purpose in the events of Leontes' lifetime. The oracle ("the King shall live without an heir, if that which is lost be not found" [3.2.134–36]) is literally fulfilled in 5.2, when the gentlemen report Perdita's reunion with Leontes. Yet the oracle's fulfillment mysteriously carries with it the queen's return, for Hermione speaks and reveals that she truly lives, only when she turns to hear Paulina's announcement, "Our Perdita is found" (5.3.121). The most dramatically expressive moment in the statue scene can be that in which Hermione addresses her daughter. Because "the oracle / Gave hope," the queen has "preserved / [Herself] to see the issue" (5.3.126–28). Hope has been literally life-preserving.

The structure of the seven ages in *Pericles* joins the role of prophecy, the bigenerational action, and the reunion motif (in *The Winter's Tale* and the other romances) in attesting to the special value these plays vest in the future. It is the future that holds the possibility of giving back "that which is lost," even when such a restitution seems to human wits impossible. Hope in this sense has less to do with personal assurance or doctrinal belief than with an orientation toward the future, one such as Paul Ricoeur points to as a kind of afterworld:

> What is finally to be understood in a text is not the author or his presumed intention, nor is it the immanent structure or structures of the text, but rather the sort of world intended beyond the text as its referent. (100)

Some such intended world awaits the characters at the conclusion of Shakespeare's romances, and they rush toward it: "Lead's the way," says Pericles (5.3.84), and Leontes intones "Hastily lead away" (5.3.155).

   These realms beyond the text could be realized with impunity in the theater, where the fictionality of events on stage was acknowledged. Shakespeare's last plays gesture toward what Frye calls "a new and impossible world," offered as a "model of desire" rather than "an object of belief" (*Perspective* 117). In the sixteenth century in England, there was gradually a decline in apocalypticism and an emergence of millenarianism, the expectation of a triumphant reign on earth (Capp 100–101). Shakespearean romance offers a theatrical corollary to the political movement. In the aftermath of tragedy's apocalypticism, the romances provide, within the confines of the theater, an image of a fulfilled earthly ideal.

5

The Tempest *and* Time's *Dissolution*

How can we call the Heav'ns un-measured,
Sith measur'd Time their Corse hath measured?
How can we count this Universe immortall,
Sith many wayes the parts prove hourely mortall:
Sith his Commencement proves his Consummation,
And all things aye decline to alteration?
—Guillaume Du Bartas, Divine Weeks and Works

"**L**et me live here ever," exclaims Ferdinand, delighted by the wedding masque, "so rare a wond'red father and a wise / Makes this place Paradise" (4.1.122–24). Michael Goldman believes "Ferdinand is speaking literally" here (143); at the very least, the remark offers an interesting context for considering Prospero's island. Pretending to misunderstand the relationships inhering between the masque, its creator, and its island setting, Ferdinand tempts himself with the notion of "paradise." In wishing to "live here ever," Ferdinand mimics a naive viewer like Christopher Sly who mistakes an onstage spectacle for reality, and sets up his home in the theater.[1] Moreover, he attributes to the "place" the delightful qualities of Prospero himself, the ruler of the island and the inventor of the masque. Forgetting or disregarding Prospero's previous harsh treatment of him, unaware of the angry "passion" that will shortly stir up his "wond'red father," clearly unable to anticipate the masque's dissolution, Ferdinand fixes in time the moment of delight by

---

1. Charles Forker also draws a connection between *The Tempest* and *The Taming of the Shrew*. Both plays "call attention to the artistic conventions and processes by which dramatic illusion is achieved. It is as though Shakespeare were asking us with one voice willingly to suspend our disbelief while inviting us with another to admire his professional skills as a technician of the theater" (136).

granting it a "place," and attributing to it sanctity. He ratifies the island of *The Tempest* as an earthly paradise.

Recently *The Tempest* has been extensively studied in connection with discussions of seventeenth-century colonialism. Paul Brown, for instance, takes a typical New Historicist stance when he asserts that *The Tempest* exemplifies "a moment of *historical* crisis" rather than "some *timeless* contradiction internal to the discourse" (48). But in these efforts to historicize the play, there has been insufficient note of how the historicity of colonialist discussions was itself deeply ambiguated by eschatological rhetoric. Mircea Eliade writes:

> The colonialization of the two Americas began under an eschatological sign: people believed that the time had come to renew the Christian world, and the true renewal was the return to the Earthly Paradise. (262–63)

So while the historical moment of *The Tempest* demands attention, we need to recognize that the moment, and our records of it, were blurred by references to timelessness. The historical crisis of colonialism occurred within a conceptual framework of paradisal or utopian expectation. The island of *The Tempest* is part of a broad tradition of marvelous gardens, encompassing the classical golden age, the biblical Eden, literary arcadias, apocalyptic New Jerusalem, the Christian heaven, and England's pride as "this other Eden, demi-paradise" (*R2* 2.1.42). Each of these "places" provides a habitation and a name for human desires. Each is postulated as a timeless zone.

Early seventeenth-century apocalypticism and millenarianism provided expectations for the advent of a timeless realm. Thus there existed an idea of the imminent conjunction of the timeless with time. The relevance of this expectation to *The Tempest* is further complicated by the double appropriation of paradise within Christian history. The term signifies both Eden and heaven, the lost estate of the past and the anticipated reward of the future. As Heinrich Bullinger wrote in 1561, "For the sinne of our firste parente we were caste out of that Paradise: and Christe is come, to the ende he might brynge us agayne into Paradise, that is to saye into high felicitie" (666–67). The concept of paradise embodies a central paradox in the Christian view of time: it suggests that hope for the future aims to recover the past.

The mutual regard in *The Tempest* for past and future, the suspension of mood between bitterness and hope, suggest that Ferdinand's epithet is correct in the deepest way: the play is specifically grounded, like the concept of paradise, upon a dialectic of loss and recovery. The dramatic action, reworking a tragic past and shaping a comic future, occupies a strangely timeless zone, in which only Prospero and Ariel are fully cognizant of time's passage. Ultimately the timeless island is abandoned, and Prospero reenters the world of flux in which he has no control—artistic or magical—over encroaching death. The play itself brings a number of dualities into equilibrium, notably the duality between time and timelessness, which Prospero essentially internalizes. In resolving antitheses within a temporal context, *The Tempest* presents a refined eschatological statement.

1

Shakespeare uses the term *paradise* sparsely—only twelve occurrences in the canon, compared with 638 for *heaven*—and he generally uses it literally, to denote a garden or park. The theologically loaded term derived from the Old Persian root *pairidaeza*, which meant an enclosed pleasure ground. The later Hebrew word *pardes* was used by apocalyptic writers to mean "the home of the blessed dead after their Resurrection," and by rabbinical writers to signify "the blessed part of Sheol where the good souls awaited the Resurrection" (Giamatti 11–12). The understanding of Old Testament *paradise* as both Eden and home of the blessed dead was conflated with New Testament usage of Greek *paradeisus* as heaven. Early Christians took Luke 23.43, "to day shalt thou be with me in Paradise," to suggest immediate ascension of the dead to celestial paradise; such usage was supported by Paul's equation of "Paradise" with "the thirde heaven" in 2 Cor. 12.2–4.

According to the *OED*, the earliest recorded English usage of *paradise* is in translation of Luke 23, and hence conveys the New Testament sense of heaven. Around 1175 the word was used to refer to the Garden of Eden. By the time of the Renaissance, the word referred multivalently to primal bliss, final reward, or a place like paradise. Some Protestant theologians found they could replace purgatory, in effect, by following rabbinical tradition and indicating by *paradise* an intermediate state where the departed awaited final judgment. Jeremy Taylor describes it as "a state of peace and excellent delights" ("Funeral Sermon" 548); the Latin *refrigerium* ("refreshment") denotes "comfort, but not the full reward; a certain expectation, supported with excellent intervals of joy" (554). To Taylor the truth of this usage is

> evident in the entercourse on the cross between Christ and the converted thief. That day both were to be in paradise; but Christ himself was not then ascended into heaven, and therefore paradise was no part of that region where Christ now, and hereafter the Saints shall reign in glory. ("Funeral Sermon" 547)

Taylor interprets Christ's use in this exchange of the word *day* strictly, as a twenty-four hour period, in accordance with conventional readings of the patristic creation narrative. In each case, cosmic time is anthropomorphized. Paradise is similarly conceptualized. As a realm of perfection, it is timeless in essence but inevitably bound to chronicity by the temporal perspective of those who imagine it. Its fluid temporal moorings allowed *paradise* to suggest both the tragic chords of the loss of human felicity and the comic strains of a hope for redemption. The fluidity could be perceived as ambiguity between the image of perfection and its reality. Donne, for instance, believed that "Heaven, the end of the gospel, was represented in Paradise," but he was careful to distinguish between the eternal, uncreated home of God and its temporal image (*Sermons* 10: 51, 8: 231).[2] Donne's distinction was not universally shared, however; most saw the recurrence of paradise at time's beginning and its ending as a significant framing and hence containing of history within eternity.

When sixteenth-century voyagers described their discoveries

---

2. The temporal paradox contributed to the idea of the illusory false paradise, such as Spenser's Bower of Bliss. Embodying "the split between what seems and what is," the false paradise "looks like the image of all a man thinks he has sought in his spiritual wanderings, but in the end it is the scene wherein he learns he was wrong; where he learns that his inner wishes were only the illusions a man creates for himself" (Giamatti 88). Given this much potential for ambiguity about paradise, one can perhaps understand Shakespeare's near avoidance of the term.

as "paradisal," they demonstrated the distinct fluidity of the concept: "Englishmen impatient for [the] advent" of the New Jerusalem, acknowledging the unattainability of Eden and Arcadia, shifted their perspective from a religious, historical axis to a secular, spatial one and sought their golden world across the Atlantic (Levin 8, 184). In a sense these Renaissance voyagers were merely transferring a mythical conception of England herself to a new location across the sea. From antiquity, Britain's physical remoteness, temperate climate, and fertile soil had suggested that it was the lost island of the blessed, the counterpart in classical literature of the biblical Eden (Bennett 114–25). The tradition was renewed during the sixteenth century, when England seemed a haven of peace by contrast with the strife-torn European continent. During Elizabeth's reign, the concept of the godly prince was advanced; the queen took on a crucial role for Protestants, among whom there was "general consensus that the pope was Antichrist and that the end of the world was at hand" (Capp 97). Linking their millennial expectations with the mythical idea of the fortunate isles, the Elizabethan English fastened on biblical prophecies that mentioned islands. Works by Sir Philip Sidney, John Donne, and John Bale all show this interest in island prophecies (Bennett 129).

The matrix of ideas involving the earthly paradise, fortunate isles, and New Jerusalem finds clearest literary expression in Gaunt's homage to "this other Eden, demi-paradise" in *Richard II* (2.1.42), a passage best remembered for its sentimental patriotism, but one which ends on an apocalyptic note:

> England, bound in with the triumphant sea,
> Whose rocky shore beats back the envious siege
> Of wat'ry Neptune, is now bound in with shame,
> With inky blots and rotten parchment bonds;
> That England, that was wont to conquer others,
> Hath made a shameful conquest of itself.
>
> (2.1.61–66)

Gaunt's eulogy to England as this "demi-paradise" was the vision sixteenth-century voyagers dispatched geographically to the New World. The apocalyptic element implicit in his speech also figures importantly in Shakespeare's own depiction in *The Tempest* of a remote island paradise. Ferdinand's vision of paradise precedes by only a few lines Prospero's revels speech, which predicts the end of all things. A paradoxical link between the wish to "live here ever" and the expected dissolution of "the great globe itself" (4.1.153) is inherent in the play's vision of time. This duality between permanence and imminent dissolution affects the play's structure and its mood, and it dictates the significant decisions of Prospero.

2

Repeatedly in *The Tempest* creativity is countered with destruction. Each of the subplots climaxes with a masquelike spectacle: the betrothal masque, the vanishing banquet, and the glittering limetree are each created only to be quickly obliterated (Gordon; qtd. in Kermode, "Introduction" lxxivn). The pattern of creation-destruction pervades the structure and idiom of the play. Prospero calls up the storm, then disperses it. He begins to weave a narrative spell, recounting the loss of his dukedom, but breaks off repeatedly (Magnusson 54–55). He plots the initial attraction between Miranda and Ferdinand, then dashes their hopes. Each event looks desperate or hopeful, depending on which stage in its bifold pattern one focuses upon. Several characters call the lability of mood to our attention. Miranda's question, "What foul play had we, that we came from thence? / Or blessed was't we did?" (1.2.60–61), acknowledges the dual complexion of Prospero's opening narrative. Gonzalo balances the royal party's "hint of woe" against "the miracle" of their "preservation" (2.1.3–7). Ferdinand, once again applying to the environment words more appropriate to Prospero, attributes his survival to the paradoxical nature of the seas: "Though the seas threaten, they are merciful" (5.1.178).

The structural and thematic antinomy provokes two basic critical reactions. One involves emphasizing one or the other of the play's two poles. Thus *The Tempest* was for Coleridge an "almost miraculous" drama (138), ranking among the ideal plays (130), while Jan Kott views it as "the most bitter of Shakespeare's plays" (21), and Robert Hunter finds that "more than any other of Shakespeare's plays, *The Tempest* insists strongly upon indestructibility of evil" (240–41). The lines in this particular tug-of-war dissolve all too easily into reflections of personal attitude. Like the concept of paradise, *The Tempest* can evoke either nostalgia or hope or both. The choice between the two responses is primarily a matter of perception. The other standard approach to the play attempts to stabilize the text by discovering an encompassing pattern. This approach is traditionally associated with conservative critics such as Tillyard, who finds in *The Tempest* a regeneration of the tragic pattern, or Traversi, who sees a symbolic pattern of reconciliation. The stabilizing approach has been called into question in an age disinclined to view Shakespearean (or other) texts as stable or orthodox. Yet ironically, the counterstress on the unstable, conflict-ridden nature of Shakespeare's plays is in its own way an encompassing pattern, as many of its proponents recognize.

The problem of critical approach illustrates the fundamentally dialectical core of *The Tempest*. Hence the usefulness of Barker and Hulme's call for reading the text "with and within series of *con-texts*" (194–95). Barker and Hulme advance the concept of discourse, "the *field* in and through which texts are produced," as an approach to the play: "As a concept wider than 'text' but narrower than language itself . . . [discourse] operates at the level of the enablement of texts" (196–97). Successful examinations of *The Tempest*'s contexts have recently identified some particular dialectic: Paul Brown, like Barker and Hulme, writes of legitimation of authority; John Gillies develops the paradoxical images of temperance and fruitfulness inherent in the play; John Bender identifies a religious polarity enacted within a "fundamentally secular" play (243). Bender correlates *The Tempest* with All Saints' Day, the day on which the play was first presented at court in 1611. He traces analogies between the text and appointed scriptural readings, which illustrate "Judaic wrath," "Christian redemption," and "their combination in apocalyptic eschatology" (243). In pointing to the apocalyptic framework of All Saints' Day as a context for *The Tempest*, Bender presents an encompassing pattern which is nevertheless fundamentally paradoxical: apocalypse describes the collision of existence and nothingness. In its attempt to define and hence to contain the collision of history and eternity, apocalypse offers itself as an image of resolution. *The Tempest* functions in a similar way, offering itself as the artistic resolution of the numerous oppositions and polarities inherent to human existence and to its representation on stage.

3

The action of the play pauses climactically at the end of act 4, after Prospero reports to Ariel:

> At this hour
> Lies at my mercy all mine enemies.
> Shortly shall all my labours end. . . .
>   (4.1.262–64)

In one of many interrupted actions, Prospero and Ariel both exit and immediately reappear; the Folio text marks the apparently original act division. Upon returning to stage, Prospero reiterates the achievement of his plans:

> Now does my project gather to a head:
> My charms crack not; my spirits obey; and Time
> Goes upright with his carriage.
>   (5.1.1–3)

The hiatus in an action that could have been played continuously effects a pausing on the brink; "Now," "at this hour," Prospero expects an end to his labors. Although he seems perfectly aware of the hour, he seeks confirmation from Ariel ("How's the day?" [5.1.3]), repeating an earlier exchange:

> *Prospero.* What is the time o' th' day?
> *Ariel.*
>   Past the mid season.
> *Prospero.* At least two glasses.
>   (1.2.239–40)

Ariel's reply now sounds apocalyptic:

> On the sixt hour, at which time, my lord,
> You said our work should cease.
>   (5.1.4–5)

The cessation, predicted in their first discussion and expected throughout the play, will now occur shortly, not actually "on" but at the conclusion of the sixth hour. The pattern implicit in this prophesied end to labor mimics that of the biblical creation narrative, in which God rests after six days of creative labor, and that of the Seven Ages scheme, in which God rests after six ages of earthly history. At this point in *The Tempest*, with the action trembling on the edge of finality, Prospero, pricked on by Ariel, significantly chooses to reject "vengeance," and then draws himself up to the full height of his creative (and oratorical) energies as he releases his art in a final virtuoso display of power.

Prospero enacts a godlike role through his ability to foresee the end of his labors, as well as through his rigid control over use of time and his vision of the dissolution of "the great globe itself." He "savor[s] as much of Judeo-Christian divinity as dramatic credibility will allow" writes John Bender (242–43). The prophetic center of the play resides within Prospero, in contrast to *The Winter's Tale* or *Cymbeline*, where the center is attributed to some extrahuman force (the oracle or Jupiter). The cosmic overview attributed to Gower in *Pericles* also belongs to Prospero. These divine capacties are complicated by Prospero's manifold roles in the play. He is not simply an oracle or God or a prophet or a poet resurrected from the dead, although as magician he is partial surrogate to each of these roles. His magic, which can be taken up and put down, allows him access to power, and hence to prophetic and godlike identities. But the instability of his magic and the suspicions it inevitably provokes insidiously undermine Prospero's role as theatrical divinity. *The Tempest* presumes the role of controlling deity and the capacity to present the deity on stage but reflexively questions both.

Prospero's magic renders him intrinsically double. He is at once self (the man Prospero) and other (the capacities endowed by his magic). Prospero's identity is further complicated by the degree to which he is identified with the island. When Ferdinand grants to the island the attributes of its ruling magician, he confuses figure and ground, or character and setting, but the problem is not unique to Ferdinand. The island figures in a dreamlike way as almost an extension of Prospero's own body. The perfection of his rule is evinced by

the extent to which this world is controlled by Prospero and is even at times indistinguishable from him. The elements obey him; natural forces are an extension of his will, an external manifestation of his mind, and have, consequently, explicitly human qualities like pity and gratitude. (Orgel 369–70)

Virtually everything one can say about the island, and perhaps even about *The Tempest* as a whole, will be to some extent also about Prospero. Because of the omnipresence of Prospero in the play, private and public actions are difficult to distinguish. The main character displays almost no private side; rather, his private concerns are the specific subject of the total action.[3] When Prospero chooses forgiveness, declaring that "the rarer action is / In virtue than in vengeance" (5.1.27–28), he combines events occuring separately in *Cymbeline*. Posthumus learns forgiveness through a personal epiphany—the dream vision of his lost family. Then, in the final scene of the play, when Posthumus extends pardon to Jachimo, he inspires Cymbeline to announce blanket amnesty. These two episodes occur in distinctly contrasting arenas, the privacy of Posthumus' prison cell and the public recognition scene at the play's end. In the course of *The Tempest*, however, Prospero undergoes only one significant internal alteration—his turn to forgiveness—but it is supremely important for the others on the island. Yet this event takes place in the virtual privacy of Ariel's company, further complicating the play's merger of the private and the public. Prospero at once externalizes his self-recognition and internalizes the play's resolution.

We might well suppose that Prospero dominates *The Tempest* to the extent that ordinary differences between public and private are voided because of Shakespeare's personal investment in the hero of this late play. Since *The Tempest* features the rare instance of a plot invented by Shakespeare himself, his apparently intense involvement with the central character is especially intriguing.

4

Paradise is a socially constructed form of wish fulfillment, which corresponds on the individual level to the formation of private fantasies. Freud establishes a connection between original creations (like *The Tempest*) and childhood fantasies: both are composed in response to unsatisfied wishes, and both develop

3. Ruth Nevo comments that "the inner dimension of *The Tempest* is actually less veiled or occulted than in the other romances because we are privy to the protagonist's will and intentions from the start" (143).

from memories of early satisfaction. Freud locates artistic creativity at the juncture of memory and desire, because "we can never give anything up; we only exchange one thing for another. What appears to be a renunciation is really the formation of a substitute or surrogate" ("Creative Writers" 145). The act of creativity is placed in a liminal zone between past (memory) and future (desire).

Freud goes further to link fantasy with a third significant time, the present:

> Mental work is linked to some current impression, some provoking occasion in the present which has been able to arouse one of the subject's major wishes. From there it harks back to a memory of an earlier experience (usually an infantile one) in which this wish was fulfilled; and it now creates a situation relating to the future which represents a fulfilment of the wish. ("Creative Writers" 147)

The fantasy world is, in Freud's estimate, produced directly in response to the human experience of time as a linear sequence. Time marches resolutely from the past, through the present, and into the future, but the individual's desires are endlessly repetitive. The creative process—writing a fiction or producing a fantasy—aims to fulfill desires by recovering the past or molding the future. The apparent escape from linear time afforded by fantasy is therefore delusive, since the created world not only arises from but is itself strongly characterized by a struggle with temporality. Freud essentially perceives a dialectic in the creative process between time's forward movement and the retrogressive habits of human desire. His model resembles that inherent in the culturally created concept of paradise, whose recurrence at time's beginning and ending testifies to the way "we can never give anything up."

Prospero appears omnipotent for most of the play. Events on the island are in effect the magician's realized fantasy, and they bear the sort of relation to time that Freud observes. The "provoking occasion" is the proximity of Prospero's enemies:

> By accident most strange, bountiful Fortune
> (Now my dear lady) hath mine enemies
> Brought to this shore.
>   (1.2.178–80)

The occasion awakens several of his "major wishes." He then "harks back to a memory of an earlier experience." The action proper of *The Tempest* opens with Prospero's account of how he lost his dukedom—a memory that encompasses both the fulfilled and fully enfranchised state he originally enjoyed and its subsequent loss. The magician's task is, using Freud's terms, to "[create] a situation relating to the future which represents a fulfilment of the wish," a situation which is achieved when Prospero says:

> They being penitent,
> The sole drift of my purpose doth extend
> Not a frown further.
> (5.1.28–30)

If this were a simple wish-fulfillment fantasy, Prospero would be triumphant. Instead, he "is himself tested by the drama he has imagined" (Nevo 146). The play chafes at the edges of its comic framework; Prospero will leave the island, give up Miranda, release Ariel, and relinquish control. The fantasy is complicated by Prospero's awareness of time.

Because Prospero functions to some extent as Shakespeare's fictional substitute, we need also to consider *The Tempest* as a Shakespearean fantasy of paradise. In this analysis, the present situation or "provoking occasion" is the historical circumstance of early seventeenth-century colonialism. Reports of New World voyagers spawned the fantasy of a realized paradise, geographically distant but contemporaneous with Renaissance England. These reports drew upon the cultural memory (itself fantastical) of John of Gaunt's Edenic England. Shakespeare constructs in *The Tempest* a model of fulfillment, located in the dramatic time of the theater rather than in the future. This model collides at the play's end with the linear progression of history. Prospero's exit from the island effects an escape from the atemporal zone of fantasy into the "real" time of Milanese politics. The eschatology of the "great globe" speech implicates both fantastic and actual time.

As David Grene notes, "It is one of the most remarkable effects of *The Tempest* that a play which is an uninterrupted story of success for its chief actor leaves one with the prevailing sense of melancholy and failure (100). By the play's end, Prospero has dismissed his magic and his attendant spirit and has given his daughter to Ferdinand. Although partially muted by notes of

97

wonder and thankfulness, the resonance of loss in the final scene is very strong. Prospero's plan to "retire" to "Milan, where / Every third thought shall be my grave" (5.1.312), expresses the Lear-like truth that the loss of one's daughter and one's domain (the island over which Prospero extends absolute control, as distinct from Milan where his authority is political and therefore circumstantial) prefigures loss of life itself. Prospero's thought of his grave harkens back to the Boatswain's words in the opening scene:

> If you cannot [control the storm], give thanks you have liv'd so long, and make yourself ready in your cabin for the mischance of the hour, if it so hap. (1.1.23–26)

The two reminders of mortality frame the play. The opening storm that occasions the Boatswain's remark is in a sense a false start, for the storm's destructive force is invalidated as soon as Prospero's control over it becomes evident. Yet the magician's demonstrated power uncannily answers the Boatswain's command, with its implied choice: either control the storm or prepare for death. Prospero "allay[s]" "the wild waters" (1.2.2) and demonstrates control over the island and everyone on it, yet at the play's end he nevertheless departs to prepare for his death.

Control is the essence of the magician's art. Prospero demonstrates extreme precision in orchestrating movements on the island and carefully using the passing minutes to achieve his purposes. But despite the technical prowess that can deliver a ship "tight and yare, and bravely rigg'd as when / We first put out to sea" (5.1.224–25), when it was broken to bits three hours earlier, that can render the shipwrecked courtiers' garments "rather new dy'd than stain'd / with salt water" (2.1.64–65), that can indeed put "at [Prospero's] mercy all [his] enemies" (4.1.263), his magic has not and cannot overcome the linear progress of time.

Behind Prospero's passionate and practiced abilities to shape events in accordance with his wishes, time flows intransigently forward toward its conclusion. Miranda must, in the way of daughters, leave him; by arranging her marriage, he manipulates the specifics of an event whose actual occurrence defies his control. Each of Prospero's projects—recovering his dukedom, wresting apologies from Antonio and Alonso, betrothing Miranda to Ferdinand—exerts control over the future, but the concomitant fact of this ordered future is his own death, the corollary of Miranda's maturity and the inevitable conclusion of even the happy retirement he anticipates. His magic enacts fantasies of omnipotence, but ultimately Prospero sets aside his power, recognizing its inadequacy in the face of death. Like any art, Prospero's magic offers a stay against mutability, a seeming immortality. Like many other old artists, Prospero finally abandons the pretence of artistic immortality to stare death straight in the face. Still, in granting his mortality only "every third thought," he persists in maintaining a modicum of control, regulating his awareness of death if he cannot regulate its actuality.

5

Although he posits an inevitable recurrence of specific wishes, Freud sees fantasy as mimicking a linear temporal structure, with "past, present, and future" "strung together," like beads, "on the thread of the wish that runs through them" ("Creative Writers" 148). Considered simply, the dramatic structure of *The Tempest* follows such a sequential chronology, beginning with an account of the past, moving through the afternoon's events on the island, and closing at the point of projection into the future, with Prospero promising "calm seas, auspicious gales, / And sail so expeditious" (5.1.315–16). Yet the play's structure complicates, and partially transcends, the chronological sense of time. To all its inhabitants but Prospero and Ariel, the island seems timeless; the visitors temporarily enter a zone where ships are reconstructed in a few hours, clothing is literally renewed, lost children are recovered, and all that fades suffers "sea-change / Into something rich and strange" (1.2.401–2).

The better part of act 1 is filled with Prospero's rehearsal of events that occurred twelve years earlier. Although a prologue to the play's subsequent action, this narrative also serves as epilogue to those crucial tragic events that would, in a more loosely structured play like *The Winter's Tale*, compose the first half of the action. Prospero's epilogue, similarly, is on the one hand a traditional plaudite, the performance's last word, and on the other, a prologue to subsequent imagined action—Prospero's return, devoid of magic and requiring relief "by prayer" (16), to Naples. Sandwiched between a prologuelike opening, which functions like an epilogue, and an actual epilogue, which functions like a prologue, lies the play's appropriately Janus-faced action. Uphaus observes that "the epilogue and prologue, respectively associated with past and future, also serve as brackets enclosing Prospero's present performance of the play and its peculiar emphasis on present time (95). Kott calls the hours of performance "the time of transformation," noting that "in Renaissance symbolism three hours stood for a 'vestige of the Trinity,' three parts of Time, and the unity of Past, Present, and Future" (24). Within this timeless zone, Prospero's two major tasks concern the past and the future: punishing and ultimately forgiving his offenders; and preparing to return to Naples and arranging Miranda's marriage.

Even though he stands at the play's core, Prospero is revealed primarily through his manipulation of others. The intense demonstration of individual involvement with his community is what C. L. Barber calls "relationship by identification." This type of interaction is

> less familiar from our conscious social experience than relationship to people as objects, because it is less accessible to observation. We observe our objects, but people whom we take into ourselves by identification are matter less for our observation than for our conservation. (192)

But we can observe on stage what may elude us in our own lives: the degree to which interaction with other people constitutes individual identity. Prospero rights his past and forms his future not through increased self-awareness or personal resolution but by directing his private drama. The other players, most importantly Ariel and Caliban, are the "others" standing closest to Prospero's "self." He conducts these relationships through distinctly temporal manipulations, habitually reminding those around him of their past misdeeds, while holding out the dual-edged sword of threatened punishment or promised reward.

The pattern is initiated with Ariel's complaint, "Let me remember thee what thou hast promis'd," "remember" "thou did promise" (1.2.243, 247–49), repetition emphasizing the temporal idiom: "remember," "promis'd," "remember," "promise." Prospero responds by making Ariel himself "remember":

> Dost thou forget
> From what a torment I did free thee?
> (1.2.250–51)

> Hast thou forgot
> The foul witch Sycorax. . . .
> . . . Hast thou forgot her?
> (1.2.257–59)

> I must
> Once in a month recount what thou hast been
> Which thou forget'st.
> (1.2.261–63)

The repetition lends almost ceremonial weight to what he says is a monthly task, the acknowledgment of Ariel's subservient history. Prospero concludes:

> If thou more murmur'st, I will rend an oak
> And peg thee in his knotty entrails till
> Thou hast howl'd away twelve winters.
> (1.2.294–96)

It is a threat to repeat the past but counterbalanced by the promise that "after two days / I will discharge thee" (1.2.298–99), a promise Prospero holds out to Ariel at intervals throughout the play and makes good in the closing lines.

Aspiration to be free motivates Ariel, but Caliban, in Prospero's estimate immune to hope or inspiration, is prodded with threats of physical punishment: "Thou shalt be pinch'd / As thick as honeycomb" (1.2.328–29); "I'll rack thee with old cramps / Fill all thy bones with aches, make thee roar" (1.2.369–70). Interestingly, Caliban's memory serves him well. He knows that he "first was mine own king" (1.2.342), acknowledges his attempted rape of Miranda, and admits that his language lessons taught him "how to curse" (1.2.364). Infantile and earthbound in his desires, Caliban lives in close connection with his past, while Ariel, the aspiring spirit, is oriented toward the future. ("Creatures of an inferiour nature are possest with the *present*," writes Donne. "*Man* is a *future Creature*" [*Sermons* 8: 75]). In his treatment of each servant, Prospero acknowledges temporal progression with the memory-threat motif.

In the simplest sense, Prospero does no more than recognize

the effectiveness of threatened punishment and promised reward in guiding behavior. Yet despite the familiarity of the method, it signifies more than Prospero's skill as a manipulator. The recurrent motif of reminder, threat, and promise, verbally reiterated throughout in the echoing "remember," "forget," "promise," illustrates how temporal adjustment—coming to terms with the past, preparing for the future—is the play's central concern. A Renaissance sermon by George Gifford on Revelations 22.13 (a text read each year on Saint John's Day) shows how promise and threat imply an eschatological pattern:

> I am Alpha and Omega, the beginning and the ende, the first and the last. . . . When wee heare of great reward promised at the comming of our Lorde. . . . [and] Also when the threatning is uttered against the evill doers . . . it is despised, and neglected, even as if it came but from a mortal man. . . . And herein because we are dull, marke how the promise and the threatning are againe repeated. (443)

Reward and threat form the basic idiom of future-directed existence in general. But the concepts have peculiar relevance to the Last Judgment, when the secrets of human behavior would supposedly be revealed in all their significance.

Admonishment is used most spectacularly in *The Tempest* when Ariel appears "like a harpy" before the "three men of sin" (3.3.52–53). Ariel provides "an accurate interpretation of the past as prologue to what is now about to be" (Peterson 230). His explicit purpose is to remind and threaten: "But remember / (For that's my business to you)" (3.3.68–69). Recalling their crime against Prospero, threatening "ling'ring perdition" (77), he indicates how crucial memory is—because they have forgotten to remember their treatment of Prospero, the court party have lost integrity. Alonso has lost his son as well, but he sees no connection between the two events until Ariel asserts a pattern of meaning. Immediately it seems to Alonso manifested in nature itself:

> Methought the billows spoke, and told me of it;
> The winds did sing it to me, and the thunder,
> That deep and dreadful organ-pipe, pronounc'd
> The name of Prosper; it did base my trespass.
> Therefore my son i' th' ooze is bedded. . . .
> (3.3.96–100)

With the island speaking as Prospero, Alonso and his mates achieve contrite self-knowledge, and Prospero's purpose for them is accomplished. The motif of reward and threat has Christian resonances. Remembering what one is and has done suggests confession; the dual inducement of threatened punishment and promised reward suggests the eschatological choice between damnation and salvation. Moreover, the discovery of meaningful connections between separate episodes in a lifetime demands the sort of cosmic overview that *Pericles* incorporates. But any temptation to read Prospero's role allegorically, to see him as the God of the play, is compromised by the eventual extension of the pattern of memory, reward, and threat to the magician himself. Moreover, in abdicating his magic, Prospero indicates a certain keen ambivalence about the task of shaping the future. Because he is self-conscious and self-aware, he recognizes his human inability to play God, even within the confines of the island. He abandons the role of judge and extends the eschatological choice to himself.

The masque, the occasion for Ferdinand's vision of paradise, is interrupted when Prospero remembers that he "had forgot" the plot of Caliban, Stephano, and Trinculo to murder him. Like Alonso hearing in the winds and billows "the name of Prosper," he is recalled to knowledge once owned but now slipped away; the repressed returns. What Prospero remembers is not a past action or condition; he remembers what he had failed to anticipate—a plot against his life. In effect, he remembers his mortality. Time catches up with his art, and in fact overtakes it.

The broken masque stands as an emblem of the impossibility of playing God, of escaping mutability even through art, and Prospero stunningly endorses that

> we are such stuff
> As dreams are made on; and our little life
> Is rounded with a sleep.
>   (4.1.156–58)

Nevertheless, he is "vex'd," his "old brain is troubled" (4.1.158–59). Hillman, advancing an allegorical reading of Caliban and Ariel as figures for "the traditional soul-body dialogue," identifies Caliban with Prospero's "mortal part" ("Romance" 154; see also 141–42). Prospero's marked irritation with Caliban throughout the play comes into sharp focus under a Neoplatonic interpretation. That he is "vex'd" by Caliban's conspiracy shows his revulsion from the inescapable fact of his mortality, which at the end he finally acknowledges—"this thing of darkness" (5.1.275)—as his own. Caliban as "thing of darkness" figures the intractability of the death-bound body.[4] In the course of the play, Prospero moves from an almost total disregard for physical existence, allying himself with his airy spirit, scorning the base appetites of Caliban, to an ambiguous valuation of the body. His reunion with his brother and the king shares some of the physical emphasis of the reunions in *The Winter's Tale* and *Pericles*.

> For more assurance that a living prince
> Does now speak to thee, I embrace thy body
> (5.1.108–9)

Prospero says to Alonso, who wonderingly replies, "Thy pulse / Beats as of flesh and blood" (5.1.113–14).

The corollary of Prospero's acceptance of mortal existence, from a Christian standpoint, is forgiveness of his enemies. As "one of their kind" (5.1.23), he can neither afford nor maintain the authority necessary for vengeance. He releases his "purpose" and ceases the self-appointed task of shaping the future. The questionable implications of that endeavor have already been demonstrated. Although their violent method is much cruder than Prospero's refined tactic, Sebastian and Antonio essentially parody his purposes when they plot

> to perform an act
> Whereof what's past is prologue, what to come
> In yours and my discharge.
> (2.1.252–54)

Their presumption presents little true danger on Prospero's island, yet it highlights the magician's own desire to transcend time. Prospero abandons the project because he fails—his mor-

---

4. Meredith Skura deconstructs the critical discourse on colonialism, showing that *The Tempest* "expresses not an historically specific but a *timeless* and universal attitude toward the 'stranger'" ("Discourse" 53). She attributes Prospero's rage against Caliban to a crisis of encroaching death, "a crisis that awakens the old infantile narcissistic demand for endless fulfillment [represented in the play by Caliban] and the narcissistic rage and vengefulness against a world that denies such satisfactions" ("Discourse" 67).

tality catches up with him. Only after considering Ariel's suggestion, "if you now beheld them, your affections / Would become tender" (5.1.18–19), does Prospero gain ethical insight into his presumption. The melancholy tone of the conclusion suggests that, while Prospero manages to abdicate assumed command over the future (his own and others'), he still desires such command. He has internalized the tension between time and timelessness. The play thus "creates a situation," to return to Freud's terms, "which represents fulfilment of the wish," but the wish— to transcend time through magic, mortality through art—is finally caught in equilibrium with the reality of past, present, and future.

6

Many English people expected the world to end in 1588. John Harvey, acknowledging the likelihood of "a *Tragedie* . . . as hath not often beene plaied upon this mortall stage, and fraile *Theater*," nevertheless maintained

> that this *88.* shall at the uttermost prove but the *Prologue* thereof . . . not many yeeres hence, there may perhaps, some shrewd *Epilogue*, or at least some perillous issue of such troublesome and tragicall actes, finally be expected. (130)

Harvey's description acknowledges the theatricality of the Apocalypse. Unlike graphic or plastic arts which freeze time, drama depends on temporal fluidity for its realization; implicit in theatricality is the imputation of process. Hence, in the *theatrum mundi* metaphor, the tragedy of apocalypse contains a prologue, an epilogue, and (apparently) intervening acts. History's conclusion paradoxically occurs through a historical process.

Because Prospero, as hero, creator, and partial God in the play, merges the boundaries of personal and universal affairs, his acknowledgment of his own imminent (or even eventual) extinction is implicitly apocalyptic. The end will come, even to Prospero, who has removed himself from the tragic world of state affairs and created a haven where he directs change. *The Tempest* expresses a yearning to transcend time through art, a desire that ultimately contents itself with fixing a studied gaze on personal and cosmic destruction.

The interrupted masque signals the collision of two forces: the spell of artistic stability and the forward flow of time. But such a collision occurs each time a play is performed; it is in fact the unique circumstance of the dramatic mode, where the enduring text joins ephemeral theatrical context. So although Prospero himself confronts death and apocalypse, and subsequently abandons his attempt to control the future, the playwright who captures that process of abandonment in the play maintains at least an illusion (or perhaps it is a reality) of artistic permanence. Finally Prospero's art and Shakespeare's diverge, the former momentary and enduring only the hours of performance, the latter still relatively stable after four hundred years. The relationship between magician and playwright suggests art staring its reflection in the face.

The self-reflective quality of permanence mirrored in a changeable frame characterizes Renaissance uses of paradise. The concept of an ideal world, batted across the globe and back and forth through history, persistently demonstrates the stability of one thing—human desire to escape time. Prospero's island is no less a paradise for its incorporation of apocalypticism, since every ideal world contains the seeds of its own destruction, as Gonzalo's description of his utopia shows paradigmatically. The desire for permanence, born as it is of changeable human emotion and intellect, recognizes its own inevitable defeat.

6
Ideal Worlds: Utopia, Paradise, Theater

There is a more civilized form of philosophy which knows the dramatic context, so to speak, tries to fit in with it, and plays an appropriate part in the current performance.
—Thomas More, Utopia

All night I dreamt of heaven:
a blue space I drifted through, huge
enough to store everything.
      Far below
I saw this world—pearl
of great price; "Body," Love said,
"is the only boat
from which you can dive to find it."
—Gregory Orr, "Nantucket Morning / This World"

Robert Wolcomb, in a sermon delivered in 1605, pondered the variety of "names that are given to the place, where the faythful are after death." The Christian God might have one name, and that unspeakable, but his heavenly abode commanded a host of titles:

> For it is called in holy scripture sometimes a kingdome; sometimes the bosome of Abraham, sometimes *Paradise*, sometimes a place of many mansions; sometimes reste, sometymes the new *Jerusalem:* sometimes a citye. And al these titles do declare unto us the surpassing comfort which the godly receave when they are freed from this wretched worlde. (33)

Wolcomb's list illustrates the flexibility and implicit vagueness of the heavenly image. Although Renaissance theologians pondered such specific eschatological notions as the stature of resurrected bodies, they frequently professed the indescribability of the heavenly kingdom. As Robert Bolton explained it:

107

Our understandings upon necessity must be supernaturally
irradiated and illightened with extraordinary enlargement
and divinenesse, before we can possibly comprehend the
glorious brightnesse of heavenly joyes and full sweetnesse
of eternal blisse. (114–15)

Theologians repeatedly had recourse to Bottom the Weaver's
favorite Biblical verse, 1 Cor. 2.9 ("the things which eye hath not
sene, neither eare hathe heard, neither came into man's heart"),
to suggest the sensory yet extrasensory perceptions available to
the glorified understanding (e.g., Becon 189; Woolton, *Anatomie*
52v). The central problem in writing about heaven is that of
metaphor: how to describe a spiritual kingdom in earthly terms?

The metaphysical problems of description are especially relevant to the expected conjunction of heavenly and earthly realms
on Judgment Day. The Church's eschatology had been understood allegorically as early as the third century by the heretic
Origen, but the official position maintained that general resurrection and judgment would be actual events. Certainly the iconography of Judgment Day encouraged literalist notions. Sixteenth-
century paintings of the last day typically show a swirling mass
of human bodies, some in the act of rising from their tombs.[1]
These pictures were extremely popular. One graced the parish
church in Stratford; many town halls featured them; Hans Hol-
bein may even have produced an ornamental Last Judgment
medallion (Harbison 52–64, 177–83). Reformation iconoclasm
seems to have had little direct effect on images of Judgment Day,
which were produced by Protestant as well as Catholic artists.
Impressive physical images of eschatological doctrines, from late
productions of mystery and morality plays as well as from
graphic arts, must have embedded themselves in popular
thought in an age so prone to apocalyptic expectation. "Thought
is always image as well," writes Karl Rahner, "because there is
no concept without imagination" ("Hermeneutics" 344). Concepts as intrinsic to human identity in a Christian culture as
resurrection and afterlife especially depend upon images. What-

1. "Most eschatology of the medieval Christian world has a far more
immediate existence in the visual arts than in the written" (Morris 3).
Morris' study, unlike my own, focuses on icongraphy and primarily
discovers reflections in the plays of medieval Christian theology.

ever one's metaphysical assumptions, it is difficult to formulate an abstract notion of one's literal self.

Yet the Church's images of eschatology, under close scrutiny through the years of Reformation and Counter Reformation, had begun by Shakespeare's day to empty themselves of their authority as literal truth and to revert to the role of symbols. Joseph Wittreich writes: "Increasingly, the Last Judgment came to be interpreted not simply as the great climactic event at the end of history but as an event at the end of time through which to make sense of life in the midst of time" (92). Wittreich outlines the modern understanding of eschatology that was evolving in the seventeenth century. Judgment Day became a spectacular but somewhat redundant grand finale. Heaven was conceived as a site of future reunion, continuing the best of earthly existence after death's interruption. The eschatological vision of cosmic history was interwoven with the increasingly important history of individuals. Paradise became a relatively free-floating term for the fulfillment of desires.

There were certainly those in Renaissance England who maintained the literalness of Christian eschatology. Philip Stubbs, for instance, wrote that "as there is a Heaven, a Materiall place of perfect joye prepared for the Godly, so there is a Hell, a Materiall place of punishment for the wicked and reprobat" (Oiiir). John Harvey sounds strangely modern in his anxious wondering "in what minute, in what hour, in what day, in what weeke, in what moneth, quarter, or yeere, this finall conflagration, and universal fireworke shall happen" (31). But this age was characterized by sophistication regarding metaphors and images, as well as by cracks in the frame of religious authority. Accordingly, Luther and Calvin each analyzed metaphors of resurrection and judgment.[2] Donne labeled Eden and Christ images of heaven and God (*Sermons* 2: 320; 10: 51). Hooker described the relation of New Testament to Old as one of metaphors to their literal refer-

---

2. Luther insisted on the literal resurrection of Christ and of his believers, but saw the usefulness of metaphor, remarking, "What a precious artist St. Paul becomes [at 1 Cor. 15.35–38], painting and carving the resurrection into everything that grows on earth!" (28: 175). Calvin saw the "seede" of 1 Cor. 15.35 as "a certayne image of the resurrection," the "Trumpet" of 1 Cor. 15.52 as "a Metaphoricall speach" (*Commentarie . . . Corinthians* 187r, 191v).

ents (*Laws of Ecclesiastical Polity* 4.6.10; qtd. in Greenblatt, "Exorcists" 182). Bullinger understood a didactic purpose behind the use of divine metaphor:

> For this maner of declaryng invisible thyngs, by visible, is more fit to teache, more mete to move, more apt for perspicuitie, and most convenient and fitting, that things may be more depely imprinted in minde, and the lesse fall out of the same. . . . parables, Metaphores or Allegories, and visions. . . . serve for plainnes and perspicuitie. (B3r-v)

So long as the metaphors went unquestioned they probably did "serve for plainnes." But once the searchlights of analysis were turned on traditional eschatological concepts, they ceased to be a source of clarity.

Renaissance theologians who attempted to interpret last things lacked a hermeneutical approach. There was no language to suggest psychological correlates of heaven, no existential alternative tradition, no historicist perspective on the relevance of apocalypticism to the current age. Thomas Brightman went so far as to deny "that Christ will come forth in any visible forme," but he could offer no further insight into the Second Coming (*A Revelation of the Revelation* 820; qtd. in Ball 169). Robert Bolton betrayed his uneasiness about both literal and metaphysical interpretations of afterlife:

> If it [hellfire] be metaphoricall, as Austin seemes some where to intimate, and some moderne Divines are of mind: and as the *gold, pearles* and *precious stones* of the *Wall[,] Streets and gates* of the heavenly Jerusalem (Rev. 21) were metaphoricall: so likewise it should seeme that the fire of hell should also be figurative: And if it be so; it is yet something els, that is much more terrible and intolerable. (101–2)

Eschatology increasingly concerned itself with the moment of individual expiration, rather than focusing on the end of all time. As the shared images of resurrection, judgment, heaven, and hell were abandoned or metaphorized, new cultural forms answered the needs traditionally met by these four last things.

Renaissance drama arose within this particular historical and societal matrix. The theater came to approximate, in an age when doubt and faith were drawing into closer balance, many of the functions traditionally met by the Church. As Louis Montrose puts it: "A thoroughly engaging and deeply satisfying collective experience was to be had by going to the theatre to see a play" (60). The drama offered shared experiences of condemnation and forgiveness, of despair and hope. Barber writes that Shakespeare

> demonstrates the investment of feeling and need in the human family, by relation to the way that investment is made in the religious worship of God and the Holy Family. The creation of a new art form puts men in a new relation to their experience. . . . the drama [became] a new organ of culture, a *novum organum*. (195)

Shakespearean romance in particular provided alternative images of judgment (*Cymbeline*), afterlife (*The Winter's Tale*), temporal perspective (*Pericles*), and paradise (*The Tempest*). These plays illustrate Wittreich's point that Renaissance tragicomedy was a genre "emanating from, indeed sponsored by, the Book of Revelation" (83).

But the drama was only one, and perhaps not the most important, of the cultural forms absorbing energies formerly directed toward communal eschatology. In general the Reformation had endorsed temporal pursuits. Perhaps nowhere was the sanctification of earthly society more apparent than in the utopian schemes which flourished in the late sixteenth and early seventeenth centuries and whose assumptions contributed greatly to the cause of the Civil War. Utopianism primarily projects "a vision of the orderly city and of a city-dominated society," writes Frye ("Varieties" 27). Augustine had originally familiarized the image of the heavenly city in Revelations 14. Divine society was exclusive, rejecting the unjust from the community of the worthy (Adams 658–59); whoremongers, murderers, idolators find "no place for them within the holy citie: but they shall be without" (Gifford 446). Orderly civic government largely depended on authoritative rule. Thus when Donne envisioned heaven, he called it "our City, our dwelling, the place from whence only we receive our laws" (*Sermons* 5: 96). It is precisely this emphasis on *rule* that defines utopianism, for the mode assumes the perfectibility not of the individual but of human society. Utopianism

111

"accepts deficiencies in men and nature and strives to contain and condition them through organisational controls and sanctions," writes J. C. Davis (370). A central commanding authority is implicit for the exercising of such controls, and in this as well as in the society's ideality a connection with eschatology is evident—the central tenet of Judgment Day was God's assertion of final and complete authority. Even more perhaps than traditional eschatology, however, utopianism obviated the concept of the individual personality, for utopianism "tends to be suspicious of the human personality and its weaknesses, seeking always to nullify its effects, to create the perfectly impersonal system" (Davis 279). To the extent, therefore, that it fails to allow for individualism and to resolve (or even explore) tensions between self and society, utopianism provides an unsatisfactory substitute for traditional Christian eschatology.

At least part of Prospero's bitterness at the end of *The Tempest* arises from his apparent acknowledgment that Milanese political regeneration provides the only viable arena for rechanneling his dreams. The magic whose study initially cost him his dukedom provides him with nearly omnipotent control on the island; yet it cannot, as I have shown, release him from the bonds of his mortality. Only by exercising authority in a decidedly social sphere can he achieve the quasi immortality of an assured succession and a married daughter, so he sacrifices intense but limited control on the island to the practical goal of reinstatement as Duke of Milan. The revels speech suggests Prospero's millennarian sense of imminent destruction, yet his role is too proximate to God's for him to believe in God; the faith he professes in the epilogue is in human forgiveness. So he partially resolves his pessimism, as did many in the Renaissance, by directing it toward regeneration of the social fabric.

Yet the prototypical utopian in *The Tempest* is of course Gonzalo.[3] Because he is first and foremost a good courtier with overridingly political impulses, Gonzalo's ideal takes the form of a paradigm for realizing social perfection. The vision, like Sir Thomas More's, is defined by all that it eliminates: no letters, no

---

3. A. Lynne Magnusson finds a contrast between "Gonzalo's utopian fantasies and benign optimism" and "Prospero's disillusionment and benign skepticism" (55). I see any utopian scheme as qualified in its optimism.

economy, no industry, no work. As an ideal it may be placid, but it is nonetheless stultifying, as Derek Traversi notices: "The causes of strife and inequality among men are indeed to be excluded . . . but with them, as soon appears, most of the distinctive qualities of a fully human life" (226). Antonio and Sebastian comment on this reductiveness and also on Gonzalo's paradoxical plan to have "no sovereignty" in his commonwealth although "he would be King on't" (2.1.158). Gonzalo all but announces his ambivalence about the implicit prerequisite for utopia—strong central rule—with his dual wish to be king and no king. Gonzalo's scheme, presented in the play complete with critical commentary, reveals further self-consciousness in its comparison with Arcadia—Gonzalo "would with such perfection govern . . . T'excel the Golden Age" (2.1.167–68).

    The Tempest in fact presents an anatomy of Renaissance conceptions of the ideal society. Davis distinguishes utopia from four other types of ideal society, each to some degree implicit in the design of Shakespeare's late play.[4] The four types are differentiated by the way they resolve the central conflict facing a perfect society, which is the inherent tension between individual and communal desires. The most fantastic solution is that of Cockaygne, traditionally a land where no limitations of desire are necessary, for nature is endlessly replete. Caliban's memory of his days alone on the island touches on this tradition; Stephano glimpses Cockaygne when he imagines being king of the island with Miranda as his queen. A more balanced resolution of the problem of conflicting desires is that envisaged in Arcadia. Here nature's beneficence combines with a moderation of human behavior to create perfect harmony, the sort implicit in the dance of nymphs and reapers in the masque. The expectations Prospero has for the court party, on the other hand, presuppose the sort of "moral heroics" Davis sees as the chief characteristic of another sort of ideal world, the perfect moral commonwealth (370). Al-

---

4. Skura also notices that the play contains various utopias ("Discourse" 68) and suggests that Shakespeare's "desire for such utopias— the golden worlds and fountains of youth—has roots in personal history as well as in 'history' " ("Discourse" 67). In his essay on *The Tempest*, "Martial Law in the Land of Cockaigne," Greenblatt sees "a crisis of authority" played out against the background of the island's plenitude (*Negotiations* 156).

though Prospero has experienced enough evil at the hands of Alonso and Sebastian to be convinced of their inner corruption, he nevertheless assumes a sort of perfectibility in them, and his hope is rewarded—they are brought to penitence. Davis' fourth alternative, millenarianism, assumes a coming change both in people and their society; millenarianism's ideal is concerned with the "process of solution" to the extent that "it is a perfect form of time . . . rather than a perfect form of society" (31–32). In Prospero's anticipation of this ideal conclusion, one can sense both sadness and triumph.

Each of the ideal worlds glimpsed in the play, including utopia and paradise, is presented ambivalently, and each enters the design only fleetingly. The instability, and the unattainability, of these designs would provoke a much keener sense of melancholy than they do, however, if the play had any pretensions to more than a fictional framework. As it is, Prospero's magic reinforces the illusory quality of the play's considerations. *The Tempest* flaunts drama's ability to take up and then discard various available paradigms for an ideal world.

This excessive and self-conscious attention to "the managed society" (Davis 103) suggests that *The Tempest* ultimately offers itself, the drama, as the one legitimate ideal realm. The boundaries of the stage, like the limiting edges of Prospero's island, and like the heavenly city itself, mark a closed society. Within this magic circle, human behavior can be controlled, or human understanding can be illuminated. The dead can be revived and enjoy reunion. Closure can be, and must be, attained. Theater has its own eschatology.

The particular eschatological content of Shakespeare's last plays draws on the historical matrix of an age when the Apocalypse was in the air, while the traditional images of it were being recognized as mere images. The theater's adoption of these images might most simply be described as secularization. *Cymbeline* echoes the Advent lessons that recall personal mortality and reject judgment, but the play very pointedly eliminates explicit reference to the judge and redeemer whose imminent birth was the occasion for Advent. *The Winter's Tale* borrows the motif of resurrection from religious drama, but replaces Christ with a woman, counters the miraculous with strong resonances of nature's rebirth, and denies the resurrection itself with an (admittedly problematic) explanation of where Hermione has been.

114

Pericles plants the cosmic vision in the mind of John Gower, not God. The process of secularization, however, here entails no clear transference or alternation of allegiance, no simple conversion from the religious to the worldly arena. Instead, the relationship of Shakespeare's last plays with Renaissance eschatology involves a process of borrowing and redefining, a dynamic relation of refining, reconceptualizing, and reemphasizing.

Renaissance artists adopted the task of interpreting the Apocalypse, as Wittreich has established; furthermore, they lived in a political and religious climate saturated with eschatological concerns. At its most basic, communal eschatology supplies human requirements for an orderly universe, balanced perspective, and hope of personal survival. It connects the fate of the individual with that of the species, acknowledging a human sense of the self as both creature and creator of personal destiny. Shakespearean romance, with its reconstituted families, its patterns of redemption, its self-reflexive assertions of its own theatricality, its contingency on its creator, fulfills these needs in another way. Freud calls it "an inevitable result" of our feelings about death "that we should seek in the world of fiction, in literature and in the theatre compensation for what has been lost in life" ("Thoughts" 291). The theater permits its audience the luxury of temporary belief in its transparent illusions; there is no question here of distinguishing the real from the metaphorical. Debates over the objective "reality" of religion's images eventually destroyed its ideological authority. Lacking any pretensions to the Church's sort of truth, the theater provided images, illusions to believe in, however self-consciously, constrainedly, partially, and intermittently. Yet these illusions, because sanctioned by communal acknowledgment, provided liberating directions for belief.

Appendixes
Works Cited
Index

Appendix A
Cymbeline *and the Medieval Doomsday Plays*

Many Shakespearean plays conclude with apocalyptic overtones. There are implicit references to Doomsday in the final scenes of *Hamlet*, *Macbeth*, and *King Lear*. The individual dramatic features suggesting Apocalypse—closing battle, theophany, a series of revelations, judgmental action—are scarcely unique to *Cymbeline*, but the conjunction of these elements in a single play has no parallel in the canon. Similar plays exist, however, in Shakespeare's dramatic heritage: the Doomsday plays of the mystery cycles are analogous in many respects to *Cymbeline's* conclusion, and should be considered its cousins, if not its forebears.

The strongest similarity is a parallel temporal context, which in each case results in certain distinctive dramatic techniques. The historical Cymbeline functioned for Shakespeare like a cipher: important because of his position in time, but himself indistinct, and hence ripe for fictional treatment. The Doomsday plays also are defined by their temporal setting. Yet Doomsday, the event to end time, the frame of history itself, paradoxically lacks any historical reality, existing rather as a human projection. So while *Cymbeline* and the Doomsday plays derive their meaning from their historical position, both dramas are characterized by a certain temporal diffusion. Both present the paradox of being about history, yet lacking a historical narrative upon which to be based.

Cymbeline achieves an extratemporal quality through its simultaneous setting in prehistoric Britain, Renaissance Italy, and pastoral Wales. The play is about history, yet defies historical verisimilitude, insisting on its own existence as art, outside of linear time. In this, *Cymbeline* also resembles the Towneley *Second Shep-*

119

herds' Play, whose double plot correlates a comic victory of charity (set in medieval England) with the birth of Christ (set in Bethlehem, A.D. 1). The Doomsday plays also exploit a setting outside linear time. As the final episodes in the medieval panorama of Christian history, they frame the cycles' unwieldy subject matter, providing dramatic continuity through their references to preceding events. The judgmental action logically can be significant only in relation to what has gone before it: Doomsday is the coda to earthly affairs. Thus in the York Doomsday play, God delays announcing the subject at hand—judgment—until after he recounts his creation of earth, the subsequent fall of humankind, Christ's mission of salvation, and the ongoing human intransigence. The "Alpha and Omega" speech opening the Chester play provides a similar reminder of the divine plan shaping temporal history. In each cycle, Christ the judge recalls his Passion and displays the stigmata, thus drawing the past action into the eschatological arena and summarizing the plan of salvation. These references to the past affirm Judgment Day as the culmination of history and illustrate its virtual containment of the components of temporal existence.

Theophanies in *Cymbeline* and the Doomsday play enlarge the temporal context in another dimension: they indicate the intersection of the eternal divine realm with the temporal earthly one. Jupiter descends to assure Posthumus that a divine purpose shapes his life. Christ descends to reveal to humankind the culmination of his plan at work in history. Both plays treat history in a metaphysical sense.

The dramatized action of the Doomsday plays nevertheless has a specific historical relevance to each member of the audience. Although the degree of audience involvement with the cycle plays was apparently high, with the audience clearly implicated in the staging of the Passion, the Doomsday sequence most strikingly projects the members of the audience into the play's action. To acknowledge the presence of the entire human race, the Doomsday plays used universal types as characters, in contrast to the usual method in the cycles of presenting historical persons (Kolve 244). The Doomsday plays have been dubbed an "eschatological morality" (Leigh 260) and their characters indeed resemble those of *Everyman* or *Mankind.* The Chester *Judgment* most strikingly presents antithetical pairs of the blessed and damned: Papa Salvatus, Papa Damnatus, Rex Salvatus, Rex

Damnatus, and so on through a catalog of earthly occupations. The Towneley play presents humanity in its final aspect as either good or wicked, assigning the characters numbers—Primus Malus, Secundus Bonus—rather than names. The method of using universal types testifies, as Kolve points out, to an eschatological belief that on Judgment Day people would cease to be themselves and become "the moral sum of their actions" (224). And indeed, the confessional speeches of the newly resurrected dead, who identify themselves by their earthly deeds, compose the major portion of each play. The grounds of Christ's judgment reinforce the ultimate importance of earthly behavior. The saved are those who showed charity to their neighbors. The Doomsday plays reach out to include each member of the audience in the judgmental action by distilling character to its moral essence.

Cymbeline does not seek to represent all humanity on stage, although it does seem replete with ghosts from Shakespeare's previous plays. The final scene is devoted largely to the series of confessions which, like their Doomsday counterparts, attempt to reduce the extant characters to the sum of their actions. Some of the choices are antipathetic to the audience—Cymbeline's overturning of law to save his son Guiderius from just punishment, for instance, or his pardoning of Belarius. These surprising judgments are perhaps necessary to involve the audience in moral choice.

Cymbeline, like the other romances, attests to the power of forgiveness as a means to rebirth. In *Cymbeline*, as in the other last plays, it is the recovery of those believed to be dead that astonishes the audience and transforms the world for the characters on stage. Although the play's conclusion shows striking formal analogies with the medieval Doomsday plays, Shakespeare's treatment of Apocalypse reveals a fundamentally different—and much more optimistic—attitude towards the final judgment. While the medieval plays primarily exploit the terrors of judgment for exhortative purposes, *Cymbeline's* apocalypse is also the occasion for reunion.

Appendix B
The Winter's Tale *and the*
Corpus Christi Resurrection
Plays

Twenty years ago Glynne Wickham briefly mentioned the similarity between the statue scene in *The Winter's Tale* and the *quem quaeritis* ("whom do you seek?") trope in the medieval drama (264). Source study having fallen out of favor, there has been no sustained inquiry into the relationship. Yet numerous similarities between the statue scene and the resurrection plays in surviving cycle texts show how deeply ingrained the images of England's indigenous drama were in *The Winter's Tale*. Although manuscripts of many of the Corpus Christi plays were destroyed during or after the Reformation, the surviving texts of four complete cycles, plus the records or fragments extant from others, reveal strong generic resemblances that suggest a protocycle core. My intention is to show how this general impulse survived in *The Winter's Tale*, not to show direct association with any particular play.

The *quem quaeritis*, the portion of the Easter liturgy in which the women approaching Christ's tomb are addressed by an angel, is central to dramatic tradition. Most scholars agree that Europe's medieval religious drama began with dialogic reading of this bit of liturgy. The gospel writers carefully avoid describing the Resurrection itself and focus instead on various human reactions to news of the Resurrection. The intricacy of communal realization and response gives the episode its dramatic richness. The revelation of Christ's Resurrection to humankind stood at the center of the Corpus Christi cycles, which dominated England's native tradition for several hundred years and continued to be performed sporadically into the 1560s and 1570s.

The statue scene occupies a position of structural and emotional primacy in *The Winter's Tale* that corresponds very generally with the Resurrection's centrality in the Christian story. Hermione's return instances forgiveness and grants Leontes spiritual rebirth; yet "real redemption implies real initial loss," as Darryll Grantley puts it, and Mamillius and Antigonus remain dead. Grantley, who sees "the fall and redemption of man" as the "theme" of *The Winter's Tale*, traces its parallels with various morality and mystery plays. Yet he finds the resurrection of Hermione "rather different" in staging from its cycle analogues, although similar in "emotional impact" (18, 32).

In fact, the dynamics of the statue scene recall in some detail the English plays of Christ's first postresurrection appearance. Perhaps there was some medieval discomfiture with the gospel fact of Christ's first appearing to the redeemed sinner Mary Magdalene, for the play *Ludus Coventriae*, in a rare contravention of gospel, has Christ appear first to his mother. The other cycles, however, exploit Mary Magdalene's identity to emphasize the power of forgiveness, the mystery of grace. The repentant Magdalene, lamenting Christ's death, acknowledges her own guilt:

> Withoutten gylt then was he tayn,
> That lufly lord, thay have hym slayn,
> And tryspass dyd he neuer nane,
>   Ne yit no mys
> It was my gylt he was fortayn,
>   And nothing his.
>   (*Towneley* 318–19)

Leontes expresses a similar feeling of mea culpa at the opening of act 5 of *The Winter's Tale*:

> Whilst I remember
> Her and her virtues, I cannot forget
> My blemishes in them, and so still think of
> The wrong I did myself.
>   (5.1.6–9)

Moreover, there is a strong sense that Hermione's restoration exceeds Leontes' deserts. Despite his suffering—according to Cleomines, he has "perform'd / A saint-like sorrow," "paid down / More penitence than done trespass" (5.1.1–4)—Leontes' blustering rage, so different from Othello's mighty passion, marks him as too commonplace to warrant the miracle of his wife's return. The audience's nagging sense of the king's unwor-

thiness points a lesson in forgiveness, with the proffered grace
on stage surpassing our own judgmental bent.

Sheer uncertainty generates much of the power of the statue
scene. Poised between life and death, between levels of illusion
and reality, the statue—or actress standing like a statue—evokes
the disturbing sense of "intellectual uncertainty" that Freud calls
the uncanny ("The Uncanny" 124, 132). The audience's confusion is shared by those on stage, who seem overwhelmed and
happily disconcerted by the extreme realism of "Romano's"
statue. Perdita kneels to ask the statue's blessing, begging "give
me that hand of yours to kiss" (5.3.46). Paulina quickly breaks
in,

> O patience!
> The statue is but newly fix'd; the colour's
> Not dry.
>
> (5.3.46–48)

When Leontes announces, "Let no man mock me, / For I will
kiss her" (5.3.79–80), Paulina reiterates her warning:

> The ruddiness upon her lip is wet;
> You'll mar it if you kiss it; stain your own
> With oily painting.
>
> (5.3.81–83)

The statue, she suggests, has not yet passed into the perfection
of the realm of art. The primitive urge to touch when visual
evidence seems incredible echoes the *noli me tangere* ("do not
touch me") motif as it prominently appears in each of the surviving mystery cycles. In the Towneley play, Mary Magdalene begs
to kiss Christ's feet but is gently reproved. In the York version,
Christ explains that he has not yet ascended to heaven and hence
remains literally untouchable. *Noli me tangere* has been a favorite
theme for visual artists, for it probes the boundaries of physical
identity, the mysteries of death and afterlife, and the precise
ambiguities of the first Easter. In *The Winter's Tale*, delaying the
tactile evidence of Hermione's animation prolongs the period of
uncertainty.

But even Hermione's warmth fails to convince the court party
that she lives. Camillo exclaims that Hermione "hangs about
[Leontes'] neck!" (5.3.112), yet demands, "if she pertain to life
let her speak too" (5.3.113). So the proof that she is neither

statue, spirit, nor automaton comes with Hermione's address to Perdita. The speech unites Hermione's return with the reappearance of her daughter and hence emphasizes the oracle as an ordering force in the play, Hermione claiming to have "preserv'd" herself because "the oracle / Gave hope [Perdita] wast in being" (5.3.126–128). With the reunion of mother and daughter, the two forms of renewal in the play intersect: Perdita returns as "the spring to th' earth" (5.1.152), as lost children sometimes do; Hermione returns mysteriously, miraculously, when her hope is fulfilled. But Hermione's speech to Perdita indicates, at the most simple level, that she is in fact alive.

In the mystery cycles as well, speech proves the identity of the resurrected one. Until Christ speaks her name, Mary supposes him to be the gardener. In two cycles, he reveals himself by addressing her as "Mary" instead of "woman," as previously; in the Chester cycle, he asks directly, "Woman, is not thy name Marye?" (1: 486). *Ludus Coventriae* spotlights the moment when Mary's whole world is transformed:

> But jentyl gardener I pray to the
> If thou hym took out of his grave
> telle me qwere I may hym se
> that I may go my lord to have.

Jhesus
M.A.R.I.A.   *spectans*
                      Mary Magdalene

> A mayster and lorde to the I crave
> As thou art lord and kynge of blys
> Graunt me lord and thou vowchesave
> thyn holy ffete that i may kys

(334)

A similar transformation occurs in *The Winter's Tale*, for the supposed permanence of both art and death dissolves when the statue speaks.

The series of commands that awaken the statue has frequently been read metaphorically. But Paulina's phrases "be stone no more" (5.3.99) and "I'll fill your grave up" (5.3.101) can also be understood to imply that Hermione has actually been dead. Fitzroy Pyle supposes the "words have been preserved from a stage in the writing in which Hermione stood as a statue on her own tomb" (122n). Paulina calls the place a "chapel" (5.3.86), and before entering to Hermione the company passes through a "gallery" (5.3.10), evidently filled with statues, like a graveyard or a funeral chapel. Thus Wickham argues that

> it was surely Shakespeare's intention (made explicit by the fact that the statue is in the chapel and not in a garden or in the long gallery with the other objects . . .) that this particular statue should resemble the effigies which normally graced the tombs of the gentry in cathedrals and parish churches in Elizabethan and Jacobean England—painted effigies modelled from the death masks and actual clothes of the deceased. (264)

Grave effigies were one of the few forms of statuary available to Jacobean audiences as a context (Bruce Smith 2), so even without pondering Shakespeare's intentions, we can draw a connection between Hermione's statue and funerary art. When *"Hermione comes down"* (5.3.103sd), the scene suggests the iconography of Christ's Resurrection. In the visual arts, the risen Christ steps forth from his tomb to form a visual emblem of life triumphing over death. V. A. Kolve, speculating on how the mystery cycles might have filled the gospel silence about the actual moment of the Resurrection, supposes that they dramatized Christ stepping victoriously from the tomb, treading the bodies of the sleeping guards (196).

Metaphors of food and drink inevitably abound in the medieval Resurrection plays, since the Feast of Corpus Christi honored the institution of the Holy Sacrament. But given the general paucity of metaphor in the statue scene, it is noteworthy that Leontes uses a food metaphor twice:

> This affliction has a taste as sweet
> As any cordial comfort.
> (5.3.76–77)

And a moment later, Leontes says:

> If this be magic, let it be an art
> Lawful as eating.
> (5.3.110–11)

The images convey Leontes' natural acceptance of the apparently miraculous recovery and suggest the fundamental necessity of his love for Hermione. But they also recall his earlier metaphor of the poisoned cup. In act 2, Leontes was tormented by damning knowledge:

> There may be in the cup
> A spider steep'd, and one may drink; depart,
> And yet partake no venom (for his knowledge
> Is not infected), but if one present
> Th' abhorr'd ingredient to his eye, make known
> How he hath drunk, he cracks his gorge, his sides,
> With violent hefts. I have drunk, and seen the spider.
> (2.1.39–45)

His words pervert the injunction in the *Book of Common Prayer* against unconscionable use of Holy Communion:

> Saint Paul . . . exhorteth all persons diligently to try and examine themselves, before they presume to eat of that bread, and drink of that cup. For as the benefit is great, . . . so is the danger great if we receive the same unworthily. For then we be guilty of the body and blood of Christ our Savior. We eat and drink our own damnation, not considering the Lord's body. We kindle God's wrath against us. We provoke him to plague us with divers diseases, and sundry kinds of death. (*BCP* 258)

An infected knowledge, in Leontes' case, forms the corollary to an unclean heart; in both cases, the inner condition of the drinker changes the vessel to a cup of damnation. Leontes claims "knowledge" of Hermione's unfaithfulness, but the context suggests self-knowledge as the fatal factor. He mentions the poisoned cup just before experiencing a god's wrath and "sundry kinds of death." Significantly, the doctrine of unworthy reception figures prominently in the Resurrection sequences of three cycles. In Chester, Christ announces in the act of rising:

> I am very bread of lyfe,
> from heaven I light and am send.
> who eateth this Bread, man or wyfe,
> shall lyve with me, without ende.
> ....
> And who so ever eateth that Bread
> in synne or wicked lyfe,
> he receiveth his owne death.
> I warne both man and wyfe.
> (377–78)

Appendix B

Towneley's Christ delivers a longer oration, which concludes:

That ilk veray brede of lyfe
becommys my fleshe in wordys fyfe;
who so it resaves in syn or stryfe
  Bese dede for ever:
And whoso it takys in rightwys lyfe
Dy shall he never.

(316)

Depending on how it is received, the sacrament can mean either salvation or eternal death. Leontes sees eternal death dissolved with Hermione's return, which spells a kind of salvation, at least in earthly terms, for him. He might well recall images of the bread of life in this final scene, for he can now eat "lawfully," tasting "cordial comfort."

The image and idea of resurrection would have elicited from Shakespeare's audience a more complex response than it did from fourteenth- and fifteenth-century Catholics. The medieval resurrection motif offered a fairly familiar way of dramatizing the process whereby someone acknowledged to be dead is recognized to be alive. Some would argue that every parallel drawn between *The Winter's Tale* and the Resurrection plays might also be drawn with scriptural accounts. Luke's gospel even notes the fictive quality of the events on Easter morning, remarking how the women's "words seemed to [the Apostles] as idle tales, and they believed them not" (KJV; Luke 24.11)—a line that bears an odd resemblance to the self-conscious references to "old tales" that lace *The Winter's Tale* (5.2.28–29, 61–63; 5.3.115–17). But the phrase "idle tales" appears in the Authorized Version, which appeared too late in 1611 to be influential on a play first performed in May of that year.[1] The Geneva Bible renders the phrase as "a fained thing," thus implying that miracle seems more fictional than truthful, but without the suggestive word *tale*.

Gospel accounts of resurrection and postresurrection appear-

1. Although A. W. Pollard writes in his Introduction to the facsimile edition that "the Bible of 1611, being only a revised edition [of the Bishops' Bible] was not entered on the Stationers' Registers, nor have we any information as to the month in which it was issued" (32), the *Short Title Catalogue* shows that only one parish church had attained a copy, in folio, of the new Bible by the end of 1611.

ances probably did influence *The Winter's Tale;* a play so aware of seasonal rhythms might well attend to the church's great spring festival. But for the dramatic possibilities of a resurrection scene, the mystery cycles provide the clear model. Shakespeare, having grown up in the midst of England's traditional religious drama, would have read the Bible with the dramatic image in mind.

Works Cited

Adams, Thomas. *The Workes of Thomas Adams.* London, 1629.

Allen, Michael J. B. "Jaques Against the Seven Ages of the Proclan Man." *Modern Language Quarterly* 42 (1981): 331–46.

Ariés, Philippe. *The Hour of Our Death.* Trans. Helen Weaver. New York: Random, 1981.

Arthos, John. "*Pericles, Prince of Tyre:* A Study in the Dramatic Use of Romantic Narrative." *Shakespeare Quarterly* 4 (1953): 257–70.

Auerbach, Erich. *Mimesis: The Representation of Reality in Western Literature.* Trans. Willard R. Trask. Princeton: Princeton UP, 1953.

Augustine. *The City of God Against the Pagans.* Trans. William M. Green, et al. 7 vols. Cambridge: Harvard UP, 1957–65.

———. *Confessions.* Trans. William Watts. 2 vols. Cambridge: Harvard UP, 1912.

Ball, Bryan W. *A Great Expectation: Eschatological Thought in English Protestantism to 1660.* Studies in the History of Christian Thought 12. Leiden: Brill, 1975.

Barber, C. L. "The Family in Shakespeare's Development: Tragedy and Sacredness." Schwartz and Kahn 188–202.

Barker, Francis, and Peter Hulme. "Nymphs and Reapers Heavily Vanish: The Discursive Con-texts of *The Tempest.*" *Alternative Shakespeares.* Ed. John Drakakis. London: Metheun, 1985. 191–205.

Bartholomeusz, Dennis. "*The Winter's Tale" in Performance in England and America.* Cambridge: Cambridge UP, 1982.

Baxter, Richard. *The Saints Everlasting Rest: Or, A Treatise of the Blessed State of the Saints in their enjoyment of God in Glory.* 9th ed. London, 1662.

Beard, Thomas, trans. *The Theatre of Gods Judgements: Or, A Collection of Histories Out of Sacred, Ecclesiasticall, and prophane authors.* London, 1597 [1612, 1631, 1648].

Becon, Thomas. *The Sicke Mans Salve.* 1561. London, 1603 [1631].

Bede, "A Chronicle of the Six Ages of the World." *The Historical Works*

Works Cited

of the Venerable Bede. Trans. J. A. Giles. 2 vols. London, 1845. 2:219–95.

Begam, Richard. "The Narrative of Recovery: Telling *The Winter's Tale.*" Unpublished essay, 1983.

Bender, John B. "The Day of *The Tempest.*" *ELH* 47.2 (1980): 235–58.

Bennett, Josephine Waters. "Britain Among the Fortunate Isles." *Studies in Philology* (1956): 114–40.

Bentley, Gerald Eades. *The Jacobean and Caroline Stage: Dramatic Companies and Players.* 7 vols. Oxford: Clarendon, 1941–68.

Boethius. *The Consolation of Philosophy.* Trans. S. J. Tester. Cambridge: Harvard UP, 1973.

Bolton, Robert. *Mr. Boltons Last and Learned Worke of the Foure Last Things, Death, Judgement, Hell and Heaven.* 4th ed. London, 1639.

The Book of Common Prayer 1559: The Elizabethan Prayer Book. Ed. John E. Booty. Washington: Folger, 1976.

Brightman, Thomas. *A Revelation of the Apocalyps.* Amsterdam, 1611.

Brockbank, Philip. " 'Pericles' and the Dream of Immortality." *Shakespeare Survey* 24 (1971): 105–16.

Brown, Paul. " 'This Thing of Darkness I Acknowledge Mine': *The Tempest* and the Discourse of Colonialism." *Political Shakespeare: New Essays in Cultural Materialism.* Ed. Jonathan Dollimore and Alan Sinfield. Ithaca: Cornell UP, 1985. 48–71.

Bullinger, Heinrich. *A Hundred Sermons Upon the Apocalips of Jesu Christe.* London, 1561.

Burns, Norman T. *Christian Mortalism from Tyndale to Milton.* Cambridge: Harvard UP, 1972.

Calvin, John. *A Commentarie of John Calvine, upon the first book of Moses called Genesis.* Trans. Thomas Tymme. London, 1578.

———. *A Commentarie Upon S. Paules Epistles to the Corinthians.* Trans. Thomas Tymme. London, 1577.

Capp, Bernard. "The Political Dimension of Apocalyptic Thought." Patrides and Wittreich 93–124.

Carr, Joan. "*Cymbeline* and the Validity of Myth." *Studies in Philology* 75 (1978): 316–30.

Certaine Sermons or Homilies Appointed to be Read in Churches In the Time of Queen Elizabeth I (1547–1571). 1623. Facsimile ed. Introd. Mary Ellen Richey and Thomas B. Stroup. Gainesville: Scholars', 1968.

The Chester Mystery Cycle. Ed. R. M. Lumiansky and David Mills. Early English Text Society, supplementary series 3. London: Oxford UP, 1974.

Coleridge, Samuel Taylor. "Lectures on Shakespeare and Milton. The Ninth Lecture." *Shakespearean Criticism.* Ed. Thomas Middleton Raysor. 2 vols. Cambridge: Harvard UP, 1930. 2:121–40.

Cosgrove, Brian. "*The Winter's Tale* and the Limits of Criticism." *Studies: An Irish Quarterly Review* 66 (1977): 176–87.

Works Cited

Cullmann, Oscar. "Immortality of the Soul or Resurrection of the Body." *Immortality and Resurrection: Four Essays*. Ed. Krister Stendahl. Ingersoll Lectures. New York: Macmillan, 1965. 9–53.

Dante Alighieri. *The Divine Comedy of Dante Alighieri*. Trans. John D. Sinclair. 3 vols. New York: Oxford, 1939.

Davis, J. C. *Utopia and the Ideal Society: A Study of English Utopian Writing, 1516–1700*. New York: Cambridge UP, 1981.

Day, Martin. *Doomes-Day: Or, A Treatise of the Resurrection of the Body*. London, 1636.

Dollimore, Jonathan. *Radical Tragedy: Religion, Ideology and Power in the Drama of Shakespeare and His Contemporaries*. Chicago: U of Chicago P, 1984.

Donne, John. "The Exstasie." *The Elegies and the Songs and Sonnets*. Ed. Helen Gardner. Oxford: Clarendon, 1964. 59–61.

———. *Sermons*. Ed. George E. Potter and Evelyn M. Simpson. 10 vols. Berkeley: U of California P, 1953–62.

Du Bartas, Guillaume de Salluste. *Bartas, His Devine Weekes & Workes*. Trans. Josuah Sylvester. London, 1605.

Eagleton, Terry. *William Shakespeare*. Oxford: Basil Blackwell, 1986.

Edwards, Philip. "An Approach to the Problem of *Pericles*." *Shakespeare Survey* 5 (1952): 25–49.

Eliade, Mircea. "Paradise and Utopia: Mythical Geography and Eschatology." Manuel 260–80.

Eliot, T. S. *The Complete Poems and Plays, 1909–1950*. New York: Harcourt, 1971.

Erikson, Erik. *Childhood and Society*. 2d ed. New York: Norton, 1963.

Estwick, Nicholas. "A Learned and Godly Sermon Preached . . . at the Funerall of Mr. Robert Bolton." London, 1659.

Felperin, Howard. *Shakespearean Romance*. Princeton: Princeton UP, 1972.

———. "Shakespeare's Miracle Play." *Shakespeare Quarterly* 18 (1967): 363–74.

Forker, Charles R. "Immediacy and Remoteness in *The Taming of the Shrew* and *The Tempest*." *Shakespeare's Romances Reconsidered*. Ed. Carol McGinnis Kay and Henry E. Jacobs. Lincoln: U of Nebraska P, 1978. 134–48.

Freud, Sigmund. "Creative Writers and Daydreaming." Freud, *Standard Edition* 9: 141–53.

———. *The Standard Edition of the Complete Psychological Works of Sigmund Freud*. Trans. James Strachey. 24 vols. London: Hogarth, 1966–74.

———. "Thoughts for the Times on War and Death." Freud, *Standard Edition* 14: 271–302.

———. "The Uncanny." Freud, *Standard Edition* 17: 122–61.

Frye, Northrop. *Anatomy of Criticism: Four Essays*. Princeton: Princeton UP, 1957.

Works Cited

————. *The Great Code: The Bible and Literature.* New York: Harcourt, 1982.

————. *A Natural Perspective: The Development of Shakespearean Comedy and Romance.* New York: Harcourt, 1965.

————. "Recognition in *The Winter's Tale.*" *"The Winter's Tale": A Casebook.* Ed. Kenneth Muir. London: Macmillan, 1977. 184–97.

————. "Varieties of Literary Utopias." Manuel 25–49.

Geller, Lila. "*Cymbeline* and the Imagery of Covenant Theology." *Studies in English Literature* 20 (1980): 241–55.

Geneva Bible. 1560. Facsimile edition. Madison: U of Wisconsin P, 1969.

Giamatti, A. Bartlett. *The Earthly Paradise and the Renaissance Epic.* Princeton: Princeton UP, 1966.

Gifford, George. *Sermons Upon the Whole Booke of the Revelation.* London, 1596.

Gillies, John. "Shakespeare's Virginian Masque." *ELH* 53.4 (1986): 673–707.

The Golden Legend: or, Lives of the Saints as Englished by William Caxton. Ed. F. S. Ellis. 7 vols. London: Dent, 1943.

Goldman, Michael. *Shakespeare and the Energies of Drama.* Princeton: Princeton UP, 1972.

Gorfain, Phyllis. "Puzzle and Artifice: The Riddle as Metapoetry in 'Pericles.' " *Shakespeare Survey* 29 (1976): 11–20.

Gower, John. *The Complete Works.* Ed. G. C. Macaulay. 4 vols. Oxford: Clarendon, 1899–1902.

Grantley, Darryll. "*The Winter's Tale* and Early Religious Drama." *Comparative Drama* 20.1 (1986): 17–37.

Granville-Barker, Harley. *Prefaces to Shakespeare.* Princeton: Princeton UP, 1946.

Greenblatt, Stephen. "Shakespeare and the Exorcists." *Shakespeare and the Question of Theory.* Ed. Patricia Parker and Geoffrey Hartman. New York: Methuen, 1985. 163–87.

————. *Shakespearean Negotiations: The Circulation of Social Energy in Renaissance England.* Berkeley: U of California P, 1988.

Grene, David. *Reality and the Heroic Pattern: Last Plays of Ibsen, Shakespeare, and Sophocles.* Chicago: U of Chicago P, 1967.

Harbison, Craig. *The Last Judgement in Sixteenth Century Northern Europe: A Study of the Relation Between Art and the Reformation.* New York: Garland, 1976.

Harvey, John. *A Discoursive Probleme Concerning Prophesies.* London, 1588.

Herbert, George. *The English Poems of George Herbert.* Ed. C. A. Patrides. London: Dent, 1974.

Hillman, Richard. "Shakespeare's Gower and Gower's Shakespeare: The Larger Debt of *Pericles.*" *Shakespeare Quarterly* 36 (1985): 427–37.

Works Cited

———. "*The Tempest* as Romance and Anti-Romance." *U of Toronto Quarterly* 55.2 (1985–86): 141–60.

Hoeniger, F. David. "Gower and Shakespeare in *Pericles.*" *Shakespeare Quarterly* 33.4 (1982): 461–79.

———, ed. Introduction. *Pericles.* By William Shakespeare. New Arden Edition. London: Methuen, 1963. xiii–xci.

Hunter, Robert G. *Shakespeare and the Comedy of Forgiveness.* New York: Columbia UP, 1965.

James I of England. "A Speach in The Starre-Chamber, the xx. of June, 1616." *The Workes of the most High and mightie Prince James.* London, 1616. 549–69.

Jameson, Fredric. "Magical Narratives: Romance as Genre." *New Literary History* 7 (1975): 135–64.

Johnson, Samuel. *The Yale Edition of the Works of Samuel Johnson.* 15 vols. New Haven: Yale UP, 1958–85.

Jonson, Ben. *The Complete Poetry of Ben Jonson.* Ed. William B. Hunter, Jr. New York: Norton, 1963.

Kastan, David Scott. *Shakespeare and the Shapes of Time.* Hanover, NH: UP of New England, 1982.

Kermode, Frank, ed. Introduction. *The Tempest.* By William Shakespeare. New Arden Edition. London: Methuen, 1964. xi–lxxxviii.

———. *The Sense of an Ending: Studies in the Theory of Fiction.* London: Oxford UP, 1967.

Kerrigan, William. "The Heretical Milton: From Assumption to Mortalism." *English Literary Renaissance* 5 (1975): 125–66.

Kirsch, Arthur. *Shakespeare and the Experience of Love.* New York: Cambridge UP, 1982.

Knight, G. W. *The Crown of Life.* New York: Barnes, 1966.

Kolve, V. A. *The Play Called Corpus Christi.* Stanford: Stanford UP, 1966.

Kott, Jan. "*The Tempest,* or Repetition." *Mosaic* 10.3 (1977): 9–36.

Lacan, Jacques. "Desire and the Interpretation of Desire in *Hamlet.*" *Yale French Studies* 55/56 (1977): 11–52.

Lamont, William. *Godly Rule: Politics and Religion, 1603–60.* London: Macmillan, 1969.

Lascelles, Mary. " 'King Lear' and Doomsday." *Shakespeare Survey* 26 (1973): 69–79.

Leech, Clifford. "The Structure of the Last Plays." *Shakespeare Survey* 11 (1958): 19–30.

LeGoff, Jacques. *The Birth of Purgatory.* Trans. Arthur Goldhammer. Chicago: U of Chicago P, 1984.

Leigh, David H. "The Doomsday Mystery Play: An Eschatological Morality." *Modern Philology* 67 (1969–70): 211–23. Rpt. in *Medieval English Drama: Essays Critical and Contextual.* Ed. Jerome Taylor and Alan H. Nelson. Chicago: U of Chicago P, 1972. 260–78.

Works Cited

Levin, Harry. *The Myth of the Golden Age in the Renaissance.* New York: Oxford UP, 1969.

Lipking, Lawrence. *The Life of the Poet: Beginning and Ending Poetic Careers.* Chicago: U of Chicago P, 1981.

Ludus Coventriae, or The Plaie Called Corpus Christi. Ed. K. S. Block. Early English Text Society, extra series 120. London: Oxford UP, 1922.

Luther, Martin. *Works.* Ed. Jaroslav Pelikan and Helmut T. Lehmann. American ed. 55 vols. St. Louis: Concordia; Philadelphia: Muhlenberg, 1955–67.

McArthur, Herbert. "Tragic and Comic Modes." *Criticism* 3 (1961): 36–45.

Magnusson, A. Lynne. "Interruption in *The Tempest.*" *Shakespeare Quarterly* 37.1 (1986): 52–65.

Manuel, Frank E., ed. *Utopias and Utopian Thought.* Boston: Houghton, 1966.

Moffet, Robin. "*Cymbeline* and the Nativity." *Shakespeare Quarterly* 13 (1962): 207–18.

Montrose, Louis A. "The Purpose of Playing: Reflections on a Shakespearean Anthropology." *Helios* ns 7.2 (1980): 51–74.

Mornay, Philippe de, Lord of Plessie Marlie. *A Woorke Concerning the trewnesse of Christian Religion.* Trans. Sir Philip Sidney and Arthur Golding. London, 1587.

Morris, Harry. *Last Things in Shakespeare.* Tallahassee: Florida State UP, 1985.

Mowat, Barbara. *The Dramaturgy of Shakespeare's Romances.* Athens: U of Georgia P, 1976.

Muir, Kenneth. "The Problem of *Pericles.*" *English Studies* 30 (1949): 65–83.

Nevo, Ruth. *Shakespeare's Other Language.* New York: Methuen, 1987.

Orgel, Stephen Kitay. "New Uses of Adversity: Tragic Experience in *The Tempest.*" *In Defence of Reading.* Ed. Reuben A. Brower and Richard Poirier. New York: Dutton, 1962. Rpt. in *Essays in Shakespearean Criticism.* Ed. James L. Calderwood and Harold E. Toliver. Englewood Cliffs: Prentice, 1970. 368–87.

Ozment, Steven Z. *The Reformation in the Cities: The Appeal of Protestantism to Sixteenth-Century Germany and Switzerland.* New Haven: Yale UP, 1975.

Parr, Elnathan. *The Grounds of Divinitie.* 2d ed. London, 1615.

Patrides, C. A. "Renaissance and Modern Thought on the Last Things: A Study in Changing Conceptions." *Harvard Theological Review* 51 (1958): 169–85.

Patrides, C. A., and Joseph Wittreich, eds. *The Apocalypse in English Renaissance Thought and Literature: Patterns, Antecedents, and Repercussions.* Ithaca: Cornell UP, 1984.

Perkins, William. "An Exposition of the Symbole or Creed of the Apostles." Perkins, *Workes* 1: 119–329.

Works Cited

————. "A Fruitful Dialogue Concerning The Ende of the World." Perkins, *Workes* 3: 461–77.

————. *Workes*. 3 vols. in 2. London, 1608–9.

Peterson, Douglas L. *Time, Tide and Tempest: A Study of Shakespeare's Romances*. San Marino: Huntington, 1973.

Pollard, A. W. Introduction. Holy Bible. 1611. Facsimile ed. Oxford: Oxford UP, 1911. 9–38.

Pyle, Fitzroy. *"The Winter's Tale": A Commentary on the Structure*. London: Routledge, 1969.

Quinones, Ricardo J. *The Renaissance Discovery of Time*. Harvard Studies in Comparative Literature 31. Cambridge: Harvard UP, 1972.

Rabkin, Norman. *Shakespeare and the Problem of Meaning*. Chicago: U of Chicago P, 1981.

Rahner, Karl. *Foundations of the Christian Faith: An Introduction to the Idea of Christianity*. Trans. William V. Dych. New York: Seabury, 1978.

————. "The Hermeneutics of Eschatological Assertions." Trans. Kevin Smyth. *Theological Investigations*. Vol. 4. Baltimore: Helicon, 1966. 11 vols. 323–46.

————. "Parousia." *Encyclopedia of Theology: The Concise 'Sacramentum Mundi.'* New York: Seabury, 1975.

Rank, Otto. *Art and Artist: Creative Urge and Personality Development*. Trans. Charles Francis Atkinson. 1932. New York: Agathon, 1975.

Reeves, Marjorie. "The Development of Apocalyptic Thought: Medieval Attitudes." Patrides and Wittreich 40–72.

Ricoeur, Paul. "Toward a Hermeneutic of the Idea of Revelation." *Essays on Biblical Interpretation*. Ed. Lewis S. Mudge. Philadelphia: Fortress, 1980. 73–118.

Robinson, James E. "Time and *The Tempest*." *Journal of English and Germanic Philology* 63.2 (1964): 255–67.

Russell, Jeffrey Burton. *Dissent and Reform in the Early Middle Ages*. Berkeley: U of California P, 1965.

Schwartz, Murray M., and Coppelia Kahn, eds. *Representing Shakespeare: New Psychoanalytic Essays*. Baltimore: Johns Hopkins UP, 1980.

Shakespeare, William. *The Riverside Shakespeare*. Ed. G. Blakemore Evans, et al. Boston: Houghton, 1974.

Skura, Meredith Anne. "Discourse and the Individual: The Case of Colonialism in *The Tempest*." *Shakespeare Quarterly* 40.1 (1989): 42–69.

————. "Interpreting Posthumus' Dream from Above and Below: Families, Psychoanalysts, and Literary Critics." Schwartz and Kahn 203–16.

Smith, Barbara Herrnstein. *Poetic Closure: A Study of How Poems End*. Chicago: U of Chicago P, 1968.

Smith, Bruce. "Sermons in Stones: Shakespeare and Renaissance Sculpture." *Shakespeare Studies* 17 (1985): 1–24.

Spencer, Theodore. "Hamlet and the Nature of Reality." *Journal of En-*

Works Cited

glish Literary History 5 (1938): 253–277. Rpt. in Twentieth Century Interpretations of "Hamlet": A Collection of Critical Essays. Ed. David Bevington. Englewood Cliffs: Prentice, 1968. 32–42.

Stubbs, Philip. The Anatomy of Abuses. 1583. New York: Johnson, 1972.

Taylor, Jeremy. "Advent Sunday. Doomsday Book; or, Christ's Advent to Judgment." Taylor, Works 5: 1–51.

——. "A Sermon Preached at the Funeral of that Worthy Knight Sir George Dalstone, September 28, 1657." Taylor, Works 6:531–68.

——. The Whole Works. 15 vols. London, 1828.

Taylor, Michael. "The Pastoral Reckoning in 'Cymbeline.' " Shakespeare Survey 36 (1983): 97–106.

Tillyard, E. M. W. Shakespeare's Last Plays. London: Chatto and Windus, 1938.

The Towneley Plays. Ed. George England and Alfred W. Pollard. Early English Text Society, extra series 71. 1897. Millwood, NY: Kraus, 1978.

Traversi, Derek. Shakespeare: The Last Phase. New York: Harcourt, 1954.

Uphaus, Robert. Beyond Tragedy: Structure and Experience in Shakespeare's Romances. Lexington: UP of Kentucky, 1981.

Walker, D. P. The Decline of Hell: Seventeenth Century Discussions of Eternal Torment. Chicago: U of Chicago P, 1964.

Warren, Roger. "Theatrical Virtuosity and Poetic Complexity in 'Cymbeline.' " Shakespeare Survey 29 (1976): 41–49.

Wickham, Glynne. Shakespeare's Dramatic Heritage. London: Routledge, 1969.

Williams, Raymond. Problems in Materialism and Culture. London: Verso, 1980.

Wittreich, Joseph. "Image of that Horror": History, Prophecy, and Apocalypse in "King Lear." San Marino: Huntington, 1984.

Wolcomb, Robert. The State of the Godly Both in This Life, and in the Life to Come. London, 1606.

Woolton, John. A Newe Anatomie of Whole Man, as well of his body, as of his Soule. London, 1576.

——. A Treatise of the Immortalitie of the Soule. London, 1576.

Yeats, W. B. "The Circus Animals' Desertion." The Collected Poems of W. B. Yeats. New York: Macmillan, 1956.

York Plays. Ed. Lucy Toulmin Smith. 1885. New York: Russell, 1963.

Index

Cynthia Marshall received her Ph.D. from the University of Virginia. Since 1985 she has taught at Rhodes College in Memphis, Tennessee, where she recently won the Clarence Day Award for Outstanding Teaching. Her published works include articles on Renaissance funerary sculpture (in *Soundings*), on Freud's readings of *Julius Caesar* (in *Literature and Psychology*), and on George MacDonald's use of allegory (in *Children's Literature*). She is currently working on a study of problems of gender and representation in Shakespeare's Roman plays.

DATE	ISSUED TO
DEC 08 '92	

CONCORDIA COLLEGE LIBRARY
2811 NE Holman St.
Portland, OR 97211